D1547140

You may see the goal ... but do you know how to get there?

On the gridiron, the end zone represents a clear-cut destination. The challenge lies in developing — and executing — a yard-by-yard strategy for getting there. Following his conversion, winning quarterback Steve Bartkowski discovered a far more significant goal: all-out commitment to Christ. He also saw the need for a disciplined plan for moving in that direction, based on the Word of God.

Perhaps you're an avid football fan. Perhaps you don't know a touchback from a touchdown. But if you want to know what it means to be "intercepted" by the Lord Jesus Christ, you'll find out in the following pages. And through this unique spiritual biography, you'll receive a faith-stretching pattern for discipleship that may change your life.

Given in
Memory of:

Bill Coyne
Class-mate
& Football
played at
Lenoir-Rhyne
in the 50's

By:

Steve Ellett
Class '57

Steve Bartkowski

INTERCEPTED
A Game Plan for Spiritual Growth

Dan DeHaan

CARL A. RUDISILL LIBRARY
LENOIR RHYNE COLLEGE

Fleming H. Revell Company
Old Tappan, New Jersey

BR
1725
,B348
D43
1980
147864
Dec. 1989

Unless otherwise identified, Scripture quotations are from the New American Standard Bible, © The Lockman Foundation 1960, 1962, 1963, 1968, 1971, 1972, 1973, 1975.

Scripture quotations identified KJV are from the King James Version of the Bible.

Library of Congress Cataloging in Publication Data

DeHaan, Dan.
   Steve Bartkowski intercepted.

   (A Power book)
   "Originally published by Cross Roads Books under the title, Intercepted by Christ"—Verso t.p.
   Includes bibliographical references.
   1. Bartkowski, Steve. 2. Christian biography—United States. 3. Football players—United States—Biography. I. Title II. Title: Intercepted.
BR1725.B348D43   1980   280'.4'0924 [B]   81-10621
ISBN 0-8007-5075-6   AACR2

A Power Book
Published by Fleming H. Revell Company
Originally Published by
Cross Roads Books under the title
INTERCEPTED BY CHRIST

Copyright © 1980 by TCL Ministries
All Rights Reserved
Printed in the United States of America

TO the brothers in Christ of the Atlanta Falcons, who made the truths in this book come alive

Acknowledgments

Thanks to my wife, Penny, for adding richness to my writings.

Thanks to my secretary, Cheryl Russell, for guarding my office so I could study and write.

Thanks to Bob Hill for helping to edit the book.

Thanks to the Metro Bible Study of Atlanta for praying consistently for Steve and me, and for listening intently as I teach them week to week.

A special thanks to Pat Turner, for being mightily used of God to reveal to us the title for this book.

Contents

Introduction

The study of a biography is always inspiring to me, but usually it has a central problem to the serious reader. If we are not careful, we are prone to exalt the individual with appreciation rather than appropriate the truth behind the person. We must remember that we have not been told to follow in the footsteps of great characters, but in the footsteps of their great faith, because their faith is in a Person. It is this Person, Jesus Christ, that this book is committed to exalt, rather than Steve Bartkowski. The temptation to appreciate the man without appropriating the message behind the man is a common failure we want to avoid.

The middle verse in the entire Bible is Psalms 118:8. "It is better to take refuge in the Lord Than to trust in man." This book is intended to explain the truth of that great verse. Some may complain that the book does not say enough about Steve Bartkowski. I assure you that it will reveal many things about his personal life which you have never read before. But it is intended to show you something greater—Steve Bartkowski's God.

I remember very clearly the radiance I saw on the face of Steve Bartkowski when he finally understood what it meant to "take refuge in the Lord." I recall several times when he trusted in himself and tried to get free from God's mighty hand. I can also recall the disappointments that came into his life during the process. God was desiring to communicate with the young athlete, who was wrapped up in his own self-confidence. The struggle was long, hard, and demanding for Steve, but just beyond the struggle, he learned there was victory. He also learned that God's ways are not man's ways, and that to take refuge in the Lord demands that we know Him well.

My hope is that you will finish the final chapter of this book and find yourself knowing God in a greater way than before. I hope that at several points in this book, you will lose sight of Steve Bartkowski and find that God is revealing Himself to you. Unless we attain this goal, we are left with revelation, without destination. We are left with a man's testimony about God, rather than knowing God for ourselves.

It is the marvel of such a great God that we must communicate. The Word of God has said it so beautifully in these words: "Though youths grow weary and tired,/And vigorous young men stumble badly,/Yet those who wait for the Lord/ Will gain new strength;/They will mount up with wings like eagles,/They will run and not get tired,/They will walk and not become weary" (Isaiah 40:30,31).

DAN DEHAAN
Atlanta, Georgia

in the suburbs of San Francisco. Steve was enrolled in Burnett Junior High School and later transferred to Curtis Junior High in Santa Clara. His athletic abilities were immediately noticed, and when he was in the eighth grade, he was voted the most outstanding athlete in his school. Success in sports was apparent for the young athlete, yet he remembers that some unanswered problems had begun to surface in his life.

Steve had dedicated his life to sports. He had little time for anything else and was willing to give everything he had to win. He won, while inside he felt that he was losing. While his friends saw him as number one, God saw him as nothing apart from Christ. Years later, he heard a statement made by an evangelist which seemed to typify his feelings during his early teen years. Evangelist Vance Havner said "Some fights are lost even though we win. A bulldog can whip a skunk, but it just isn't worth it." The young athlete's road to success was filled with many misleading adventures, until he found life's most important quest.

As a freshman in Buchser High School, Steve's athletic ability increased even more rapidly. His life revolved around basketball and baseball, and he was fourteen years old before he played any organized football. A friend suggested that they play on the freshman football team just for the fun of it. Steve was a natural for quarterback—the right size and a good arm—so he and his buddy decided to try out for the team. During his first season in high-school football, he threw for fifteen touchdowns in six games.

While Steve still loved baseball, his father could see that it was beginning to lose its glow in the young athlete's life. For a while Roman refused to sign a parental letter of consent, allowing Steve to play football. "Why not stick with baseball," he advised. "You can't get injured as easily and you're bound to get hurt in football." What no one realized at the time was that God would use those very football injuries to bring Steve to Himself.

In his first year of high school, his team won the Santa Clara

Valley Athletic League title in basketball at the junior-varsity level. Steve made all-league and averaged nineteen points per game. He participated in all three sports—football, baseball, and basketball—during his four years at Buchser. His athletic career was off to a good start, since he made the varsity baseball team while still a freshman, a feat never before accomplished at his school. Steve credits his dad's knowledge of baseball and continuous coaching in his accomplishing this honor.

During the summer months, Roman continued to coach his son in the youth baseball league. In 1968, his team was runner-up in the Colt League World Series in Riverside, California. The following year, the team went to Lafayette, Indiana, and captured the World Series crown, which they had lost in the finals the previous year.

At this stage in Steve's athletic career, success and winning seemed to fall in place. In basketball, his team was number three in Northern California during his sophomore year. He averaged nearly twenty points a game. The amazing thing about his boyhood drive was that Steve desired nothing more than to just perform well. The trophies, awards, and praises were unimportant to him. The simplicity of a single-minded athlete, with a tremendous drive to excel, were the only things that mattered. "If only it had stayed that way," Steve recalls.

Steve was "in it to win it," not in it to win a prize or the praise of men. He was determined to win the game, but happy to lay down the fame. At this point in his life, his priority had not become a projection of his own ego.

His junior year in high school was not as easy as the first two. The innocent fun of playing ball was being taken over by the praise of men and pressures from the outside. In football, Steve was voted the most valuable back in the Santa Clara Valley Athletic League and his team was 7-2 for the season. However, basketball was his favorite sport during the year, with his team coming close to a perfect season. They finished with a 28-2 record and were ranked number one in Northern California. In one game, Steve scored 52 points. Honors continued to come his way during the years. However, the baseball team was the poorest ever. They lacked discipline and a winning attitude, even though Steve played well and continued to receive several honors for his abilities.

As a maturing teenager, Steve gave little thought to God, except to attend church on Sunday and to pray occasionally before a big game. Yet, there was a sense that God was leading him to a personal encounter with Himself. He felt he had little need for the Lord. He was too successful and too taken up with sports to acknowledge a need for a personal relationship with the Lord of life.

His senior year began with the absence of most of his friends and former teammates. Because of his ability, he had been playing a year ahead of his age and most of the former players had graduated. "We had a team of 5'5" receivers and 150-pound guards," Steve remembers. Even though they had players much smaller in stature, the team somehow managed to improve their record to 7-1-1. Steve was the biggest man on the team during his senior year and was again voted the most valuable back in the league. During his four years of football, he threw for more than 60 touchdowns. His senior year in basketball was equally impressive. He averaged more than 25 points per game.

College recruiters were taking a special interest in the graduating senior. He had more than one hundred scholarships offered in football and many basketball recruiters were also showing interest. Steve knew that a very important decision would have to be made shortly, and in a nostalgic way, dreaded to see his high-school career come to a close.

During his high-school days, Steve was very shy. Many of his classmates misinterpreted his shyness as conceit, and he remained alone much of the time. He had very little confidence in himself, except in sports. He never attended a high-school dance and did not go to his Senior Prom. Often, his mother had to encourage him to accept various awards which were given to him for his sports participation. He didn't care for the rewards. He just loved to play the game and win. He was comfortable in performing to the best of his ability and had no ulterior motives but to be successful. He was confident in his abilities and believed that the measure of his success was due to his dedication to playing his best. But God was beginning to bring about a series of events that would disturb his comfortable position in life.

Jesus Christ came to disturb the comfortable. Steve would be brought face-to-face with some stark realities that would cause him to no longer trust in his religiosity, his upbringing, or his ability. He would be shown later that the rich man in the Scriptures went away sorrowful because he was too content, while the beggar was accepted by God because he cried out in his need (Luke 18). God delights in stripping our self-confidence. He has no program to save us as long as we are depending on our own goodness within ourselves. Steve did not understand this biblical principle until several years later, when he heard the following illustration that brought the truth home to his heart.

After a series of meetings had finished, evangelist Billy Sunday was helping the workmen take down the huge tent which was used during the revival. A young man who had attended the services the night before was now greatly convicted of his sins. He approached Mr. Sunday and earnestly inquired, "What must I do to be saved?"

Billy's reply was startling. "You are too late," he said as he continued to work.

"Oh, don't say that," exclaimed the young man, "for I earnestly desire salvation. I will do anything or go anywhere to obtain it."

"I cannot help it," came the reply. "You are too late; for your salvation was completed many years ago by Jesus Christ, and it is a finished work. All you have to do is simply accept it. You have done nothing and can do nothing to merit salvation. It is free to all who will receive it."

God is asking you to receive something for which you put forth no labor, and for which you have no merit or credentials. You must receive it God's way or you will not receive it at all.

As his high-school years were coming to a close, God was beginning to move Steve closer in receiving His fullness, His way. God was also "in it to win it." God was going to have Steve give up his right to himself. However, the young athlete did not know that God's determination and victory were going to be so dramatic.

2

Opening the Chamber of Horrors

When God begins to prepare a man for an encounter with Himself, He begins by unlocking the chamber of horrors called S-E-L-F. For Steve Bartkowski, this was the beginning of a painful experience.

"As I look back now," Steve says, "I can see how God was working in every intricate detail of my life. I was completely wrapped up in sports, and winning was the name of the game for me. I felt comfortable with my life-style and confident with my athletic abilities."

God delights to comfort the afflicted, but He also wants to afflict the comfortable. When Steve graduated from high school, God began to deal with him in several specific areas, in order to get his attention. We must remember that it is not a man's goodness, or, for that matter, his badness, that makes him a candidate for conversion. Only a personal confrontation with the Lord Jesus Christ has the power to save. God gets us ready to receive such a confrontation by revealing the inadequacies of our self-life. In one He may unlock the horrors of self-righteousness. In another, it may be self-pity or it could be self-consciousness. In still another, it could be self-seeking or self-love.

In January of Steve's senior year at Buchser High, the recruiting became serious business. When Jim Plunkett, the Heisman Trophy winner, came from Stanford to talk to him about playing football for them, Steve knew that he was in the game of big-time ball. Choosing to remain close to home, he narrowed his choices of scholarship offers to three colleges: UCLA, Stanford, and California at Berkeley. After a series of checking and double-checking, he found that California was his best opportunity for quarterbacking and chose to accept the offer from the college closest to his home.

During the process of recruitment and eventual signing with Cal, Steve began to realize that playing the game for fun was over. Suddenly, football and sports became a hard, grueling, competitive sport. He began to see life as "get all you can" and "don't worry about the other fellow—think only of yourself."

When Steve entered the University of California at Berkeley, he found the school had become a haven for the radical and rebellious. The "street people" had invaded the campus and had convinced many of the students to adopt their "hang loose" philosophy. The Berkeley students were becoming the trend setters in unorthodox politics and were battling for the minds of many people. The free flow of drugs, sexual orgies, and demonstrations caused Steve to regret his decision in choosing the university, even though it was close to home.

A rule in force at the time hindered Steve from playing varsity ball as a freshman. For his first year it was necessary that he play on the freshman team and, as quarterback, completed the year with four wins and one loss. He was taken up in the fierce competition and played his best to win. However, during this time, his academic grades suffered tremendously.

One day Steve was called into the dean's office. A recruiter had told him that he would not have to worry about his grades. All he had to do was to play football and the grades would take care of themselves. Therefore, he believed that the dean would compliment him for his outstanding performance on the gridiron and ask if there were any way they could help him. However, he soon found that the reason for his visit was not football but the miserable status of his grades. He was told to shape up in his grades or else. Pressure, on and off the field, began to increase. The school was put on probation for three years for tampering with grade transcripts. This meant that the team could not participate in any bowl games and was not allowed national television coverage while on probation. Attendance at the games was usually about 30,000, while Stanford was drawing more than 70,000 at home games.

Steve began contemplating a transfer to another college. He was fed up with the pressure and his disillusionment with the university climaxed near the end of his first year. Many of his teammates were leaving the school and he felt inclined to join them. Yet, he remembered that his father had taught him not to run away from difficulties or obstacles. He had tried to live by that principle since his high-school days. He determined that he would not leave, even though the pressures and difficulties continued to increase.

Baseball was still an important game to Steve. After his high-school graduation, he was drafted by the Kansas City Royals and was offered a handsome bonus if he would sign. They encouraged him to forget about football and college studies. Baseball was fun, and he enjoyed playing on the junior-varsity team at Cal during his freshman year. He averaged more than .350 for his first year at the plate and looked forward to playing on the varsity team during his sophomore year. In his "dual" sports role, he did not have to depend on either of the sports to keep him in school. He could play either above average, which was both enviable and dangerous for the young athlete.

The excitement of football continued to grow on Steve. He began his sophomore year as starting quarterback at Cal. During the first game of the year against Colorado, he completed 24 passes out of 49 with nearly 300 yards gained, against the sixth-rated team in the country. He looked forward to the next game against Washington State and knew that it would be even better, since Washington State was not rated nearly as high as Colorado.

Adversity struck for the first time in Steve's athletic career. During the Washington State game, he dislocated his left elbow hurdling a tackler. The rule prohibiting freshman from playing on the varsity team had been lifted between seasons, and the coach brought in freshman quarterback Vince Ferragamo to replace the injured Bartkowski on the roster.

Jay Cruze was the incumbent quarterback and resumed the position after Steve was injured. However, attendance continued to decrease and the team lost several games. For three weeks, Steve sat on the bench, until his elbow healed. He was ready to resume his position as quarterback. While attendance declined, the supporting alumni applied pressure on head coach Mike White to play the freshman, Ferragamo. White conceded and began playing Vince as the starting quarterback. The freshman quarterback played well while Steve sat on the bench and watched. It was a shattering experience for Steve. It was the first time in his athletic career that he was not the starter.

Anger and bitterness began to build up inside the young athlete. He decided that he would tell the coaching staff at the end of the season that he was going to concentrate all of his energies and time on baseball. After all, he loved baseball and could excel in this sport as well as football. His decision was reached out of anger rather than wisdom.

During the spring, he played baseball and did better than ever. He shattered Jackie Jensen's single-season home-run record of 8 with 12 round-trippers. Steve also hit for an average of .345 and had several game-winning runs batted in. It was a very redemptive time for the "dual" sportsman. He could show his peers that football didn't mean as much to him as they thought.

Steve spent the summer honing his baseball skills in a small town in Kansas. His team played more than 60 games in a two-month period and finished second in the National Baseball Congress Semi-professional tournament in Wichita, Kansas. Several scouts told him that he would be a number-one baseball draft choice if he would give up football.

Still undecided about football, Steve talked to several of his teammates and with some personal persuasion from Coach Mike White, he decided that he would play football at Cal during his junior year. There was no doubt that Vince Ferragamo would be the starting quarterback. But Ferragamo had minor problems with consistency, and Steve was told that he was next in line to be called upon. When the time came, he responded admirably to the challenge. Within a short period of time, there were questions as to who would be starting at the quarterback position. No one knew who would start the next game until the last minute. Cal had developed into a two-platoon quarterback system.

Football became exciting for Steve again. The team's record for that year was a poor 4 and 7, but football had a resurgence back into Steve Bartkowski's life. Baseball during the summer months was not nearly as exciting to him, and when the draft was announced, Steve found that he was not drafted until the nineteenth round by the Baltimore Orioles. Yet, he pondered the situation and wondered if he should take the opportunity to leave football and devote his energies to baseball.

The phone rang at Steve's parents' home in Santa Clara as he was giving serious thought to the baseball draft.

"Hey, Steve, this is Mike White," the caller announced. "I don't suppose you've heard the news yet, but Vince has decided to transfer to Nebraska."

It didn't take long for Steve to realize what this meant.

"The job as starting quarterback is yours if you decide to return to Cal for your senior year," Mike offered.

The announcement by White relieved a heavy burden from Steve's mind. He decided that he owed it to himself to make one final, concentrated effort in football, maybe for the last time. That summer he put more energy into training for football than at any time in his life. Steve said, "I was the first one on the field and the last one to leave. Nothing meant more to me than being the best quarterback in the country." He was committed to go "all the way" with football this time. He had made the decision to seek this goal above everything else in life.

During his previous injury and subsequent "benching" for most of the season, God was trying to get his attention. Steve gave the situation some fleeting thought but decided that since he had the natural ability to be a good football player, he would push God out of his mind for the present and, in reality, let football become the object of his worship.

In Steve's case, it was worshiping a detour from what God was trying to tell him to worship. He determined that he would be the best quarterback in the country. He would push his natural talents to the limits. He would exalt himself to the pinnacle of excellence. But he failed to heed the warning which is given five times in the New Testament: "Humble yourselves before the mighty hand of God and He will exalt you" (see 1 Peter 5:6). Through the humiliating experience of being a second-stringer and the elbow injury, God used the opportunity to open the chamber of horrors before Steve, but the young athlete closed the door again and again. But God is patient. It was as though God were saying, "Humble yourself now or you will be humbled later."

In his senior year at Cal, Steve practically rewrote all of the single-season records in passing at the university. He made All-American for the season and football became the number-one priority in his life. He was invited to three post-season bowl games and God allowed him to continue to play his best. During his last bowl game in college football, he was awarded a new 1975 Dodge Charger for being the "player of the game." His performance during these games captured the attention of professional football scouts. Many believed that he would be among the first to be picked in the upcoming NFL draft.

During the 1975 draft Steve was elated to learn that he had

become the number one draft choice in the entire country. He later signed the wealthiest rookie contract in football history with the faltering Atlanta Falcons. Suddenly, the "pot of gold" was there and he grabbed for all he could get for himself. He had "arrived," and immediately began chasing after false and unfulfilling ventures in his adopted city of Atlanta. Although he failed to realize it, God was allowing him to enter into the horrible traps of boredom, loneliness, and defeat.

"I believe that God had a divine purpose in bringing me to Atlanta," Steve says. "It was here that I met many of His people who exposed the real condition of my heart."

In the fifth game of his first season, Steve's elbow was injured while playing against San Francisco. With cautious padding and taping, he tried to play again. But two games later, it was again dislocated. He persuaded the coach and doctors to remove the cast before the injury was completely mended, so he could return to his team and the action he loved so dearly. A specially designed brace was made for his elbow, making it virtually impossible to dislocate again. He finished the season in Green Bay, where the elbow was dislocated for the fourth time. He had missed four games during the season, yet he was voted the National Football League's Rookie of the Year for 1975.

After his first season had ended, it was necessary that his elbow receive surgical attention. Steve entered the hospital for the delicate operation; it was the first time he had ever required surgical attention for anything. "This was the most painful experience I had ever had," he remembers. During his hospital stay, and especially while recuperating at his apartment, God began to deal with "Atlanta's Golden Boy," as he was affectionately known by the local newspapers.

A spiritual battle had begun within the young athlete. God was beginning to allow Steve to see himself, a proud, self-sufficient, unbroken man who trusted in himself and his ability to succeed. At the same time, Satan continued to push him, to force him to rely upon himself, to become his own god.

Steve later learned that Satan is the master in the art of a slow approach. He is a deceiver and appeals to one's pride. He even implies that to do God's will is bondage (Genesis 3:1-5). Steve remembers two specific illustrations he had heard which show the deceptive art of Satan's slow approach.

The first was when several university professors took a frog and placed him in a pot of boiling water. The frog, still in control of his senses, immediately jumped out of the pot. Again, they took the frog and placed him in a similar pot of cool water. They turned up the heat under the pot a few degrees every few minutes. After several hours, the water was brought to a boil and the frog, becoming accustomed to the increased heat, was finally boiled to death.

"This is how the devil tries to manipulate man," Steve said. "He deceives and pushes a man until he is only a puppet of the devil's wishes. He becomes a cold and hardened shell. He slowly loses his ability to reach God and to know the abundant life in Christ."

The other illustration, which was relevant to Steve's life at the time of his recuperation, is the story of the lark and the fox. One day the fox came through the woods to speak to the lark, a beautiful bird which could soar through the air for a long time without flapping its wings.

"I have wronged you many times," the fox said. "But I have a plan to make amends for all of my tricks toward you."

"Sure," the lark replied. "I know better than to buy that line. You are deceitful through and through, and I know better than to listen to you."

"Now just listen to me for a minute," the fox continued. "That can't hurt you."

"Well, all right," the lark consented.

"Here is the plan. I will come through the woods every day and leave a fat, juicy worm on the path for you. You can watch me leave the woods and then come down to retrieve the worm," the fox instructed. "The only thing I ask in return is that you give me one of your beautiful feathers."

The lark thought for a while and then replied, "You have a deal. I can give you a hundred of my feathers and still fly."

The first morning came and the fox was right on schedule. He came with the biggest, fattest, juiciest worm the lark had ever seen, laid it on the path, and left the woods as promised. The lark swooped down, ate the worm, and left a feather before returning to the treetops. The scene was repeated daily for several months, while the lark continued to get fatter and fatter. Then one day, after the lark had eaten the worm and left his feather, he noticed that it was becoming a bit harder to fly back to the skies. Another month went by and flying was becoming more difficult every day. After ten months of this "deal" with the fox, the lark, with most of his feathers now gone, tried to get off the ground, but found that it was impossible. He flapped his wings hard, but he could not fly. The fox saw this as his moment to move in for the final kill. While the poor lark continued to try to fly, the sly fox snatched the lark and ate him whole.

Steve had met several of his teammates and other friends in Atlanta who had encouraged him to give his life to Christ. During his recuperation from the elbow surgery, he had ample time to think about spiritual things. Yet, Satan was trying to deceive him with a similar trick of slow approach. God wants his children to "mount up with wings like eagles" (Isaiah 40:31), while Satan offers us worms in place of those wings. What a pity to sacrifice wings for worms! What a pity to harden your heart when God is trying to speak to you. The Scripture says, "A man who hardens his neck after much reproof/Will suddenly be broken beyond remedy" (Proverbs 29:1). To Steve Bartkowski, it became a matter of "humbling himself now or humbling himself later." Steve's chamber of horrors was beginning to open up. He was seeing himself as God saw him—a man in need!

3

When God Won't Let Go

Several members of the Falcons had gathered for their weekly Bible study. I was especially surprised when Steve walked into the meeting and took a seat near the middle of the room. It was the first time that I had met him and I was elated that he had joined his teammates for serious Bible study. During the session I noticed that Steve was visibly moved, especially when he would periodically drop his head, deep in thought, and then look straight into my eyes as if to say, "Is this for real?"

When the study was concluded, most of the players stood around the room and chatted for several minutes before leaving for home. Steve approached me and we became acquainted.

"Dan," he said humbly. "I sure would love to get together with you sometime for a serious talk." I looked into his eyes and noticed that his statement was more than a casual remark. "God knows I am hungry," he concluded.

We agreed that a serious talk together was a joint priority between us, and deep in my heart I knew that Steve had been born again, even if he did not know it himself. On the way home that evening, I talked with my wife, Penny, about my conversation with Steve.

"I really believe that Steve is a Christian," I told her. "Even though he did not tell me, I saw it in his face."

It was during that brief encounter after the Bible study that a lasting relationship developed between Steve and me. God began to move in his life in a strange way that gripped Steve's heart like nothing I had ever seen. I could tell that there was a continuous sensitivity to what God was about to do in his life.

The events leading to his conversion were quite dramatic, and there was evidence that God was dealing very specifically with him since he moved to Atlanta to assume the spotlight on the Falcons' roster. Atlantans would watch the rise, the fall, and the rebirth of their star quarterback during the next three years, but they would not know all of the details of God's dealing in Steve's life. Many of them would not know that "Atlanta's Golden Boy" had become a Christian, but they would see dramatic change in his life.

Over the years, I have asked many people, "What is a Christian?" The answers I have received are surprising. One fellow told me that being born in a Christian country such as ours automatically made him a Christian. "Certainly," he said, "I am not a Communist or a heathen." But being born in a Christian country could not make one a Christian any more than being born in a stable would make a man a horse. If a person were born in a garage, he would not be an automobile.

Another man told me that his father was a Christian and, therefore, he was! I asked him, "Does that mean it runs in the bloodstream?" If your dad had an artificial wooden leg, would you also have one? The Bible makes it clear that God has no grandchildren.

On another occasion, I asked a man in a store, "What is a Christian?" He quickly responded, "A Christian is one who believes in Jesus Christ." Before I let him explain his answer, I asked another question.

"Is the devil a Christian?"

"Of course not," was his rapid reply.

"Well, the Bible says in James, chapter 2, that the devil believes in Jesus Christ. Does that make him a Christian?"

The fellow stood there in silence for a moment. I could tell that he was giving serious thought to my question and finally became frustrated with me and himself. Before we parted I shared with him further and came to the realization that he really did know Jesus Christ personally. But it is an error to say that one who knows Jesus Christ is one who just "believes" in Him. We could easily think that believing in Jesus is like believing in Abraham Lincoln. We may believe that Lincoln existed and that he did some great things, but what has that got to do with our salvation?

What is a Christian? It is an ordinary person with an extraordinary love for all that Jesus Christ is. A man who is not a Christian is basically a person with an extraordinary love for himself. To be set free to love the Lord Jesus Christ as we were created to do, involves a series of events where God sets us free from ourselves. When that happens, we no longer hold so dear our own selfish world. It also demands our having God's view of sin. Sin is that disposition of self-rule which makes a man an enemy of God (Romans 8:7). It is preoccupation with our self-life. It is one of the things that caused Steve to see himself as God saw him.

Steve's second year with the Falcons began with a feeling of excitement. His elbow had healed nicely and he was ready to play a full season free of injury. He felt that he had everything a young, single man could want. With plenty of money at his disposal, he fulfilled his college dreams of pampering himself with everything he had ever dreamed about. He bought a boat, a house, a truck, and anything he desired. Despite his first-year injury, the fans had voted Steve the most valuable rookie of the year, and he had received a new car along with the honor. As he began his second year, his selfish excitement was again to be thwarted by God's plans for his personal life.

Preseason training was the hardest work he had ever put into his athletic program, as he made plans for the biggest year in his career. He was ready to take on the whole NFL! However, the Falcons just could not get it together. They played very poorly during the first several games. During the fifth game of the season, Steve was grabbed by the face mask and through the drastic swing of his body, his knee was severely torn.

"Oh, no!" he remembers saying as he lay in pain on the grid-iron. "This can't be happening to me."

After being helped to the locker room, knowing he would be out of action for the rest of the season, he said, "I remember crying in the locker room down in the Superdome. I was completely baffled as to why it had happened to me. Two seasons in the NFL, two severe injuries. I would have to sit on the side-lines watching rather than playing the game I so dearly loved." His dreams were again shattered.

In January, when the cast was finally removed from his knee, he found himself extremely lonely. The season was over. His teammates had gone home, and he would go to the sta-dium alone to rehabilitate his knee. He knew that he had to get his knee back in shape again. His only choice was to "gut it out" and work on it alone. Through constant work, his knee was brought back to 100 percent strength. But other problems began to surface that he had never faced before. For the first time in his life, the young athlete was experiencing severe, per-sistent loneliness.

"How I hated to go to that lonely pit to rehab every day," Steve remembers. "To add to the complications, I was ex-tremely lonely in my private life."

This was a real switch for Steve Bartkowski. He had always been riding the wave of success and self-rule. During his school days, he enjoyed being loved and acknowledged. He enjoyed playing for the sport itself and innocently wanting to be good at what he did. Now, his whole personality was beginning to change. He was being overtaken by a drive to be what he could never be—his own god!

The Atlanta newspapers, as well as some fans, wanted to make Steve the "Joe Namath of the South." The press was writing about Atlanta's quarterback, presenting a different person from what Steve wanted. But he felt that he must con-form to what they wanted. "I was forced to live a role where I was never comfortable," he says. "The people wanted someone exciting to read about, and the pressure was on to conform to their wishes." Steve's youthful innocence, or immaturity, led him to follow their wishes, believing that it would eventually lead to the right road. He did not see the DEAD END street sign on the road which the public wanted him to travel.

It is true that all of us are prone to change with time. It is also true that if God doesn't change a man's character, people will. Steve was beginning to see his "shy, fun-loving boy image" change into a bold and hardened life-style. He tried to live the image of a superhero. The nightlife began. The chasing of material fulfillment increased. Friends who were ready to "mold him" came in abundance. The press had pictured him as handsome, rich, and free, and this image began to creep into his association with women. He was losing his own identity by living with other people's ideas about himself.

Steve said, "There was no reason for me not to be the happiest person in the whole world. Yet, there was a terrible lack of fulfillment. I thought that the next purchase of a car would fulfill me, or the next night out on the town would suffice. I honestly thought it would work.

"Maybe I was expecting too much of happiness," he continued. "Perhaps the world was right, that happiness is based on things, events, and people. I was a very lonely person during this time. In fact, I was so lonely that I asked my best friend, Mike Hodgins, to move to Atlanta from California, just to help me share some of the loneliness."

During the fourth preseason game of his third year with the Falcons, his knee slipped again while playing against Tampa Bay. Soon after that, it happened again and again. Steve was convinced that there was something seriously wrong with his knee, despite the diagnosis given by others. During practice it slipped again, and the doctors performed an orthogram on the injured knee. It was no surprise to him when the doctors announced that there was a piece of torn cartilage in his knee.

"I was crushed," Steve said. "I left that room and cried the whole afternoon. I never felt so alone in my life. It seemed like my whole life was caving in."

He was told that it would take six weeks to rehabilitate his knee. "I was out playing in four weeks," he recalls. "Everything was downhill from there." For the rest of the year, he didn't play very well. The fans were critical of him, the press was down on him, and God was allowing Steve to face the most severe year of his life.

"There was nowhere to turn," he says. "I was ashamed of who I was. I was ashamed of being Steve Bartkowski because things were going so poorly.

"I kept telling myself that I was happy. I had an abundance of things," Steve related. But even when he played a good statistical game, people were still critical. The public, as well as many friends, began to question his abilities. While he was trying to do his very best, the fans continued to be unimpressed with him. He was baffled, but God was aware of his situation and was about to make an interception in his life.

Training camp for his fourth year in the pros was extremely difficult. Steve was apprehensive about recurring injuries, and it began to shake his future. God was so clearly taking the earthly props away from Steve. He was waiting for him to voluntarily drop the props and cry out to Him. The day for Steve's conversion was approaching.

It was during the preseason game against Philadelphia, in Steve's fourth year with the Falcons, that the crash came. For a number-one draft choice, he was playing terribly. The harder he tried to play, the worse things seemed to get. "It seemed as though the dead end in my career had finally arrived," Steve remembers. The fans were booing and the press criticizing. The pressure hit the team members and it came to a climax in Steve's life.

The night following the Eagles game, Steve went home crushed from all of the events in his life. He knew he had to get alone to settle some things.

"This is it," Steve told himself. "I have tried as hard as I can in every game, and still things continue to get worse. There is nothing else I can do. I have done all I can. There is no more ability left in me."

He didn't want to talk with anyone. He was lonely, yet he didn't care to have friends over for the evening. He was miserable as he made his way into his darkened house. But that night he went home in the darkness to find the Light! He separated himself from his critical fans to find the only critic worth listening to—Jesus Christ! He walked away from his coaches to discover the greatest coach of all time. He went away alone to find a life where he would never have to be lonely again.

Alone in his room, Steve recalled that a stranger once told him how to become a Christian. He bowed his head and repeated the simple prayer. Even though he had said this prayer before, it had meant nothing to him. Now, it was taking on new meaning.

It is not the mere words a man speaks to God that makes him right with God; it is the attitude of his heart. God demands a broken heart and a humbled life. There is no other way to acknowledge sin. Very simply, Steve asked God to put His plan to work in his life. He asked Jesus Christ to come into his life and take over as number one.

"It was the last resort for me," Steve said. "I did not know what else to do. I had been through one traumatic culture shock while a sheltered boy going to Berkeley. I was about to experience another in Atlanta. I was scared," he added.

"I was not sure what happened. The only thing I was sure about was there was a terrific sense of peace that came over me as I prayed. A huge burden left me," he says. This was a miracle. To be relieved from so much pressure, and to experience a peace that unexplainable, was a work of God. "No person, except a born-again Christian, could ever understand it," Steve said. "I knew I had had an encounter with the living Lord, even though I was not sure how to explain it."

The Bible began to take on a new meaning to Steve. He found himself hungering to read and understand it. Before, it was just another book. It tasted like grits without salt, like dry oatmeal. Now it had begun to come alive. Despite this tremendous experience, Steve was not ready to say anything about it to his friends.

During the next three games, June Jones, a committed Christian, started as the Falcons' quarterback. At the end of the second game of the regular season, he spoke to Steve about getting his life right with God. Steve did not tell him about his recent conversion, but listened intently when June spoke boldly for the Lord.

"Bart" he said, "I want you to know that I am going to quarterback this team until you give your life to God."

Still, Steve did not say anything about his born-again experience. June's words sank deep into Steve's mind and confirmed again the decision he had made a few weeks earlier.

Recently, I asked Steve to relate to me the immediate signs of salvation in his life. He gave me a very clear answer because he could remember the experience so well.

"First, there was the peace and freedom from pressure for the first time ever," he said. "And the seed whose fruit is righteousness is sown in peace . . ." (James 3:18).

"Second, there was a hunger for the Word." "Like newborn babes, long for the pure milk of the word, that by it you may grow . . ." (1 Peter 2:2).

"Third, there was confidence and security that God was in control of events." "And the work of righteousness will be peace, and the service of righteousness, quietness and confidence forever" (Isaiah 32:17).

"Fourth, my life-style changed dramatically. I used to have to go out with the guys all the time. Now I was free to stay at home and not feel loneliness like before. I was free." "For you were formerly darkness, but now you are light in the Lord; walk as children of light" (Ephesians 5:8).

There is no doubt about it. Steve had been intercepted by

Christ! God used a few interceptions in his last games to point to the divine interception. It was through misery and loneliness that Steve saw himself and realized his need. The interception had been completed. Now would come the maneuverings of God, so Steve would know what it really means to win!

4

Running a Race We've Already Won

Shortly after Steve's conversion to Christ, several members of the Atlanta Falcons, who were also Christians, began to encourage him. June Jones, one of Steve's closest friends, shared a Scripture portion with him that has become a favorite. "Be anxious for nothing, but in everything by prayer and supplication with thanksgiving let your requests be known to God. And the peace of God which surpasses all comprehension, shall guard your hearts and your minds in Christ Jesus" (Philippians 4:6,7).

Greg Brezina, who has been affectionately called the spiritual daddy of the team, had a profound influence in Steve's new life. "He has such a stable and consistent walk with the Lord," Steve believes.

The new life which Steve found in Christ brought several changes in his daily habits. He found that there was truth in the statement, "A Christian can do anything he wants to, because God changes his *want to's.*" Early in his new life, God began to change his desires. Yet there were many things he never had to change because God took away his "want to" in doing them. The power of God became a reality. He knew he was owned, bought, and paid for by Jesus Christ! The security of belonging to the family of God began to bring peace into his life.

One of the problems which Steve had concerning his new life was a long-standing misconception about Christianity. He had come from a fairly religious background, had gone through a major culture shock at Berkeley, had let the world push him into its mold, and as a result, had arrived at several misconceptions about Christianity.

One fallacy Steve had was that to become a Christian meant that you give up your right to do anything. He honestly believed that the Christian must resign from all activity and excitement. "I thought that I would have to give up all those things I had bought and earned over the years. I did not realize I only had to wait on God to take the desires away from me," he said. It was very pleasing to watch God at work in Steve's life—giving and taking away certain desires. Those of us who watched his development were thrilled by Steve's growing security in the Lord.

"Dan, the Lord has spoken to me about tithing," Steve told me one day.

"Oh, really?" I replied.

"What is tithing?" Steve asked, as I tried to keep from laughing.

He knew he was supposed to tithe, even though he wasn't sure what it was. This was a degree of the sensitivity which God was working in him.

Another misconception Steve had in his past was about Christianity itself. For all he knew, Christians were an unorganized group of people belonging to a cult. He was unsure what would happen if he were to join them. He did not know the basics of Christianity. He had never understood the principles of the Bible on discipleship to a living Lord. His past, somehow, had resulted in a fragmented view of God, Jesus Christ, and most assuredly, the Holy Spirit.

Steve also shared with me the misconception he had about other Christians. Most of the ones he had observed were just plain "weird." Now, some of his former friends think he is weird, and he has a burden to relate the truth about this misconception to those he loves. Many of his close friends are still living the life that Steve used to live, and are finding loneliness, boredom, and futility as constant companions.

It is easy to see the problem many people with a religious background have with Christianity. Most of them have already been filled with extrinsic motivation. They have learned the principles, but there has been no intrinsic or inward motivation to apply them to personal behavior. Without the personal relationship to Christ, "religiousness" is just rules without learning. It sometimes takes longer to break through to one who has had many rules to live by, than for one who has had no religiosity. Remember, the problem in denying Christ is self—either self-righteousness or self-condemnation—but it is still self.

But God had already won that victory in Steve's life. Now he was learning what it meant to be a servant. A servant is one who, recognizing God's sovereign will, leaps to do that will of his own free choice. Even today, Steve knows that God has an unchanging plan for him, yet his security in that knowledge does not hinder his "leaping for the Lord" in working out that plan.

In most spiritual circles today, the emphasis is on the *work* rather than the *workman*. One of the greatest lessons Steve was to learn was that the Christian life is much more character than conduct. It is a life of "being," not a life of "doing." While many sincere Christians encouraged Steve to "hit the road for Christ," he was learning one of the great lessons of Christianity. The central truth about the kingdom of Jesus Christ is a personal relationship with Him—not public usefulness to men.

Since his conversion to Christ, I had made it a practice to give Steve some choice books. I would hand him two books at a time and tell him to read them for "going-to-bed stories." It was exciting to watch him grow and to depend upon God for his security.

One of the first books I gave him was *The Pursuit of God* by A. W. Tozer. If you have read this thrilling book, you already

know that it would stretch any new Christian. Steve began to
have a sincere hunger after God, not in just doing things for
God. He was learning that God's Person is much greater than
Steve's performance. The one would automatically result in
the other. If he knew God's person better, his performance
would be greater.

A second book I gave him was *How Come It's Taking Me So
Long to Get Better?* This book had a powerful impact on Steve.
It set him free from the guilty feeling that he had to be giving
his testimony every week. From reading the book, he understood the reason many new Christians remain "child prodi-
gies" spiritually. They run ahead of God. They try to do a
work for God without being secure in God. They seek their security in an activity, rather than in God Himself. There is
probably no greater danger to the new Christian. God taught
this important principle beautifully to Steve.

Early in his conversion, Steve refused an invitation to talk to
a group of doctors who wanted to hear his testimony. Confident that it was not God's will for him, he told the group that
he was not quite ready. He believed that the day would come
when God would use him in public ministry, but for the present, it was not His will.

Steve was learning to run a new race, and God wanted to
share His riches with him to make him secure in all that he had
in Christ. I remember telling Steve that we Christians have
been guilty of telling new converts to "stand up, stand up for
Jesus." What we need to tell them is to "sit down, sit down
with Jesus." God has so much to share with a new Christian
that no Bible teacher or preacher could ever share. Many
times, we teachers try to tell new converts the full cycle of their
responsibilities. We push them to attend three Bible studies a
week and get them started on the "Christian circuit." Then we
wonder why they cannot handle the pressure of standing up for
the Lord. What we should teach these new Christians, especially the celebrities, is that they are to be comfortable in their

knowledge of God before they seek comfort from a public ministry or other people.

One great advantage a person who is secure in God has is that he will know the difference between when God is speaking to him about something and when men are trying to twist his arm. This is a desperate need today! Even our view of sin today, by most people, shows that they have heard too many preachers and have heard too little from God Himself. Every view of sin, except the biblical view, looks on sin as a disease, a weakness, a blunder, an infirmity. The Bible revelation shows sin to be an anarchy, not a missing of the mark, but a refusal to aim at the mark.

God calls sin exactly what it is, but He also supplies the remedy for it in equally precise terms. Steve was learning that man calls sin an accident, while God calls it an abomination. Man can do something about an accident. Only God can cure an abomination. Man calls sin a blunder; God calls it blindness. To cure a blunder we need more light for our path. But all the light in the world will not help a blind man to see. He needs sight, not light. Man calls sin infirmity; God calls it iniquity. Man will try to cover up a problem. Only God can cover up moral guilt. Man calls sin reasonable by saying, "We all do it." God calls sin rebellion!

Another valuable lesson Steve was learning was that the entire Christian life demands that we have a heart for God. Our performance before others might impress them, but God can see through the veneer and knows our motives and actions. A man who knows God, and is secure in what he has in Christ, will always be a God-conscious person. He is then free from being intimidated by others, because he has seen God's view of himself.

Steve began the long road to know God, and to know His will for his life. He began to call sin what God called it, and not as other Christians might view it. He began to read a man's heart more than his head.

In the early days of his conversion, Steve found himself trying to imitate some of the older Christians he had met. He soon realized that a man who abides in Christ is free from trying to imitate righteousness. Today, there is little emphasis given to "abiding in Christ," while great emphasis is given to "do this" or "do that." Steve began to realize he could not do anything that did not become, in the rugged language of Isaiah, "like a filthy garment" (Isaiah 64:6). No matter how good it might look, if it were divorced from "abiding in Christ," it was just more filthy rags. I advised Steve to think seriously about everything he did and to ask himself the following question: "Is this work, this activity, deflecting you from abiding in Christ? If so, throw it overboard!"

Many who call themselves Christians are not really devoted to Christ. They may be devoted to the Christian life and live it out of habit and they may also exercise their natural virtues for the sake of Christ. You remember, Peter did this with his expert sword-flashing ability. He thought he was using his abilities for God's purposes when he cut off the ear of an enemy. All he really did was give Jesus another cleanup job.

God is not looking for men to help Him. He is looking for men who know Him so well that they find themselves serving the Lord unconsciously. They are no longer *trying* to serve the Lord, they just get on with it! They no longer say, as children, "Look, I'm doing it!" They just do it, and whether or not people notice is of no concern to them.

This was a major lesson for Steve Bartkowski to learn. Like many others, he went through a period of finding that God did not need his natural abilities. God can, and does, go far beyond the natural.

Our natural virtues may break down because they are not promises of what we are going to be, only remnants of what we once were, remnants of the man God made and sin ruined. It may be that when someone is naturally patient, after being born again, he may become impatient. If someone had been pure, upright, and worthy before conversion, he may begin to have thoughts of evil such as he never dreamed before. Steve learned that Jesus Christ did not patch up his natural virtues. He created a new man. "Therefore if any man is in Christ, he is a new creature; the old things passed away; behold, new things have come" (2 Corinthians 5:17).

He also learned that character is developed during crisis. No crisis is greater than during a period of time when God is hacking away at us, while we are trying to serve Him in the flesh.

For sure, when Steve Bartkowski was converted to Christ, he was a baby. I knew he was born again, but I also knew that he was very easily impressed as a new Christian. I was afraid that many people would try to teach him that the Christian life is fulfilled in doing something. They might teach him that the victory was still to be won, that it would depend on Steve Bartkowski whether it was won or lost. No, No, No! My friend, the victory is already won (2 Corinthians 2:14).

One of the first books Steve read was *How Come It's Taking Me So Long to Get Better?* The author, Lane Adams, said:

> I'm not suggesting we wait eighteen years to ordain people to the ministry, but rather that we learn to gauge maturity by Bible standards. We must allow enough time for individuals to mature before saddling them with heavy responsibilities.
>
> When my daughter, Susie, first went to school, I remember on one of my visits there seeing a boy about six years old whose eyes were brimming with tears and whose chin was beginning to quiver. You could see he was terrified. His father took one look at him and in a very stern and severe tone said, "Be a man!" The one thing a six year old boy can't be is a man. No way. He's a six year old boy, and he has a right to be frightened at the prospect of all the strangeness of school.
>
> Yet, for centuries this is what we have been shouting at our feeble little babes in Christ. Worse yet, we teach them

to shout it themselves. No wonder so many live under constant burden of guilt and self-accusation. It takes time, and Paul's life is an outstanding example of this. How good, though, that his life also exhibits the unlimited patience of a loving, heavenly Father.

5

The Danger of Drifting

After several in-depth sessions of learning to "rest in the Lord," Steve was ready for the next building stone in his new-found life. But, this new lesson would be a bit more difficult to learn! Like many new Christians, as well as several older ones, there is a constant pressure to drift away from the Lord.

Shortly after Steve's conversion to Christ, I began teaching a regular Bible study for several members of the Atlanta Falcons and their wives. I felt impressed to teach the important steps in spiritual drifting. About fifteen of the players and their wives attended regularly, and I believed that for some reason, God wanted me to share these principles with them.

It was apparent God was blessing Steve abundantly after his conversion. On the field, he continuously became a better player. He began the regular season that year by sitting on the bench for the first two games. But by the end of the season, the faltering Atlanta Falcons had reached the play-offs and just narrowly missed the Super Bowl by a close loss to the Dallas Cowboys.

Because of Steve's new freedom in the Lord, a new freedom on the gridiron was created. The whole team could see a change in Steve Bartkowski. The press wrote about it, Atlantans talked about it, and I prayed about it. I knew that he would be swamped with well-wishing Christians wanting him to speak and make appearances across the country, but the press was baffled. They wanted to know the reason for his flashback into being the real pro, which was evident during the final game of the season. They couldn't buy his relationship with Christ as the determining factor. All the while, God was confirming to Steve that He was in control, but pressure from people had become very real.

The constant stress made Steve avoid people as much as possible. His once revered value of the public and the press continued to decline. While I could see his reasoning, I felt that prolonged absence from other people could result in spiritual harm.

The season had been a terrific high for Steve. First, his new life in Christ and second, one of the greatest seasons in Falcon history, coupled to provide him with a feeling that he thought would never leave. I don't believe he thought it would ever wear off, but I knew it would. The off-season began in a flash. Steve's teammates were gone, his fellowship with other Christians was gone, and the excitement of football had vanished. He decided that he would spend several months at his home in California, and that long trip home became a long stretch of drifting.

Fortunately, the drifting pattern Steve experienced was not as severe as that of many Christians. "I went home thinking that this spiritual 'high' would never wear off," Steve told me. "I no sooner got home and I found that I was lost without the fellowship I had in Atlanta. I began to get progressively lazy. Finally, I felt the glowing and growing of my Christian life had been choked off."

Nearly four months went by before Steve and I got together again. He shared with me the process in his spiritual walk during his stay in California. It was beautiful to hear him say that God had used his fiancée, Sandee Oliver, to change his thinking on the need for fellowship.

I suppose some of the reason for Steve's temporary drifting pattern was my fault. I had spent so much time drilling into him the need to have time alone with God, and not with people, that the proper balance was not perceived. The spiritual lessons we learned from Steve's drifting were invaluable for both of us. It is necessary for these lessons to be shared with others if they are to see the direction and tragedy that spiritual drifting can work in their lives. No man can drift and not be hurt. However, God can use the time to bring insight into many areas of spiritual growth. It depends on how far the drifting goes as to how bad he is hurt.

The Bible records the events of men who drifted, such as David, Lot, and Saul. While David made quite a comeback, Psalms 51 and 32 are a tribute to the agonizing hurt he experienced.

What is drifting? It is taking the easy way out! It is slowly moving in the wrong direction. It is dying by degrees. The end is certain, but the way there may be ever so slow. Drifting usually begins with carelessness. We simply fail to pay attention and we get lazy. This may lead to a curiosity for sin. When we are careless, we get curious, and if we fail to stop the pattern, we will have contact with sin. After the contact, we usually go to conniving and then we find ourselves living in carnality. From carelessness to curiosity—from curiosity to contact—from contact to conniving—from conniving to carnality.

A study of David's fall into the sin of adultery and murder will show this progression. He became lazy, then curious. He decided to make contact with sin, then tried to connive his way out of it. Finally, he lost his desire for spiritual things.

"I knew I was drifting after the first step," Steve told me. The first step does not seem so bad, but it leads to the second. Number two may not seem so bad, but it leads to the third. As we progress through these steps, the dangers continue to increase.

I remember the day I took my first group of guys down a fast-moving river in Georgia on a raft. I had studied the river carefully, but I was unaware there was a ten-foot waterfall just a mile from where we put in. We began to drift leisurely, until I heard the noise of a giant locomotive. Suddenly, I knew it was not a train, after looking ahead and seeing nothing but treetops. I yelled back to the six guys with me to bail out! They immediately responded and before I knew it, I was going over the falls with six empty rafts. Later, I thought about that illustration as to how the devil deals with God's children. He gets them started in some harmless event, especially one that appeals to the five natural senses, and then gets them moving faster and faster into terrific danger.

Steve knew that the first step in drifting for any Christian was LAZINESS. It is the little things in life that account for most of our laziness, because life is made up of accomplishing many little things. If we get lazy in the small things, it leads to bigger ones. The Christian life is similar. Laziness was one of the primary things Paul warned young Timothy about. Laziness is the number-one enemy in the Book of Proverbs. Wisdom and discipline are constantly found together in the Scriptures.

A test for laziness in our lives can be found by asking the question "Do I often find myself doing what is difficult and undesirable, just to stay in shape?" The man who is not a Christian does as he pleases. Anything that rubs against his grain is usually discontinued very quickly. If he is not paid for it or if he cannot see any immediate results for his own good, then he just quits. Watch out for laziness! This was the first danger signal Steve failed to heed and it led him to the second step in the pattern of drifting (2 Timothy 2:3,6,10).

The second step is LACK OF PURPOSE or BOREDOM. Laziness always opens the door for boredom in the Christian life. God never intended for our lives to be filled with apathy or to be lacking in purpose. Spiritual guidance in the Christian life is a result of having our eyes on the goal and not on people. It also involves obeying the duty that lies nearest. But how many of us have obeyed the small part of God's truths that we already know? It is here that we usually stumble because of laziness and then question God for our lack of purpose. A good test for this second step is to ask yourself, "Can I create ways to stay in shape spiritually without the help of anyone else? Am I able to take a few minutes and make them count spiritually?" (Proverbs 6:6–11 and Hebrews 6:11,12).

Step three is RESTLESSNESS. This is the usual result of step two. When a person becomes bored, he begins to get restless. Try as he will to do something about his boredom, he usually will do the wrong thing. This adds sin to sin. " 'Woe to the rebellious children,' declares the Lord, 'who execute a plan, but not Mine, And make an alliance, but not of My Spirit, In order to add sin to sin' " (Isaiah 30:1). The test for restlessness is, if you were alone for two days without any communication, radio, television, or telephone, could you make vital use of your time without going crazy? Many people today cannot be alone for an extended period of time. Even some teenagers cannot study without headphones clamped to their ears. They are restless! (Proverbs 8:34–36 and Exodus 14:10–12).

The fourth step in the pattern of drifting is SELF-PITY. When a person becomes restless, without some given task to do, he can very easily slip into this fourth area of drifting. Then begins the "pity party." "Poor, poor me!" you may hear him say. Self-pity, like every other kind of selfishness, is nothing short of having one's eyes completely focused on oneself. At this point, the Christian has lost sight of where God wants him. He is wandering and wavering in his own Christian life. A test for this step is, how long does it take you to get over some wrong another person has done toward you? (Proverbs 16:32).

PRIDE is the fifth step. It naturally flows from the previous step. If drifting continues, then self-pity will lead to self-proclamation! The latter is much more intensified. It results in a life consumed in being concerned about what others think of you rather than what the Lord thinks of you. To test your response, ask yourself, "Do I find myself easily angered?" If so, you have some rights which were never given up to the Lord. Also ask, "Do I find myself compromising on what I know to be right, just to please the crowd?" (Exodus 34:14 and Proverbs 28:25).

The sixth step is MURMURING. It is misery to be in the

company of a person with a complaining attitude. Just being around them is depressing. Their attitude reveals a heart completely filled with pride, and when we are filled with our selfish ways, whatever does not please us, we begin to murmur against it. Murmuring is a sin! When constantly in use, it will keep the light of Christ from shining through. The test is, how often do you find yourself wishing things were better? Exodus 16:8 and Numbers 11:1 tell us that all murmuring is a denial that God is sovereign. You see, God could have changed the situation, but chose not to. When you murmur against it, you are saying that God made a mistake. Only a drifting person would accuse God of sin!

IMPURITY is the seventh step in the drifting pattern. Impurity is a lust after anything. It can manifest itself in the form of lusting after possessions, position, pleasure, or people. Lust is a false drive within a man. The moment he reaches his lustful goal, a new void is placed in his heart. The vicious circle continues until the man is exhausted. Usually, he will repent when he reaches the end of the road, but much damage has already been done. The test for this step is, what do you find yourself thinking about during free moments? What are the three greatest desires of your heart right now? The answer to these questions will reveal the purity of your heart.

Step number eight is A HATRED FOR REPROOF. A lustful person cannot be reprimanded rationally. He will put up his guard each time you attempt to bring up his sin. If he is not determined to leave his drifting, he will hate the reproof you offer and will even hate you for reproving him. A test for this step is, what is your attitude toward strictness or chastening? Do you always rebel or do you see it as from God?

The ninth step is BITTERNESS, RESENTMENT, AND A CONDEMNING ATTITUDE. After despising reproof, it usually follows that we get bitter. The Bible always calls bitterness a "root." Once it is in a person's heart, it will take time to remove. If God removes it quickly, it is like tearing something out by the roots, and this produces a great amount of pain. The test for this step is, do you have a constant pessimistic attitude toward life in general? How sad it is to see someone going through life with a constant pessimistic attitude, when God has created so much for our enjoyment. A bitter individual will break your heart and he is only one step away from some very severe chastening.

The final step in the drifting pattern is A HARDENED HEART. This is the last step where God's patience was shown toward the children of Israel. After this came their death in the wilderness. This was the last step in Saul's life before he committed suicide. The test for this step is, are you totally insensitive toward the Holy Spirit? The Spirit of God can no longer speak to such a person about his sin because he is hardened. He will not let God break his heart! Why would a man die without knowing Christ as personal Savior and Lord of his life? It is because he is hardened against the Lord!

My friend, God always uses broken things. The Bible is filled with illustrations of how God honors brokenness. If your heart is broken, it is a sure sign that you are open to God. Remember, the little boy's fish and loaves had to be broken before the five thousand could be fed. The woman's alabaster box had to be broken before the perfume pervaded the house. Jesus said, "Take, eat; this is my body which is broken for you" (*see* Matthew 26:26). God always uses broken vessels. On the other hand, God often chooses not to use the mighty, the rich, and the knowledgeable. He could use them, but often their pride and bitterness and their hardened hearts disqualify them from even listening to the Lord's Word.

Psalms 51:17 says that God *will not* despise a broken and contrite heart. Contrast that verse with Proverbs 29:1: "A man who hardens his neck after much reproof *will suddenly* be broken beyond remedy" (my italics). The choice is yours. God will never reject a broken spirit. You will have to let him break yours if you have been drifting. On the other hand, if you choose not to let Him break you, God has promised that you will be broken soon—but without any remedy.

Let me relate an illustration about a young boy who shot and killed a man while gambling. In those days, murderers were sentenced to hang. But the townspeople were so concerned for the young lad that they gathered a petition asking the judge to pardon the boy. Finally, the judge agreed, but only on one condition: The judge himself would wear a clerical garb and carry the pardon between the pages of the Bible. As the judge approached the boy's cell, he could hear the young man cursing and swearing at him. "Get out of here, you blank preacher."

"But son," the judge replied, "You don't understand."

"I understand fine," said the boy. "I don't want what you have to offer."

The dejected judge left the jail and later the guard told the boy that it was the judge who was dressed in the clerical garb. Between the pages of the Bible was an authorized, sealed pardon for his release. When the day of execution arrived, just before they put a black sack over the boy's head, they asked if he had anything to say.

"I am not dying because I killed a man," the young boy said. "I am dying because I rejected the pardon."

We might reject God's pardon because we think we are too good, or because we think we are too bad. Our fault before God is not necessarily our sin—He made a remedy for that! Our fault before God is rejecting the pardon. To accept it demands a broken and contrite heart. Let God break your heart.

John Wesley's mother wrote these significant words to the great preacher: "Whatever weakens your reason, impairs the tenderness of your conscience, obscures your sense of God, or takes off the relish of spiritual things—whatever increases the authority of your body over your mind—that thing to you is sin."

Steve looking for open receiver in game against New York Giants.

Left: Steve at six months, already prepared to play football. *Below* Helen and Roman Bartkowski with Steve at two years old, and sister Terri.

Left: Steve and his mother when the Bartkowskis lived in Iowa. *Below:* Steve at age five, with his father and dog "Shep."

Steve at age six—going on sixteen. *Below:* Steve at age six, with his sister Terri.

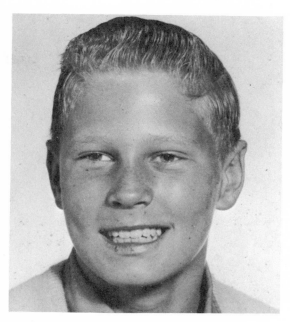

Above: Class picture, age ten. *Left:* Steve at age five, in front of his home in Iowa. *Below:* Steve at age eight, with his new bicycle.

Above, left to right: Steve (age twelve), Grandmother, Terri, and Nancy. *Below, left to right:* Terri, Nancy, and Steve (age thirteen).

Above: Steve at sixteen, observing his new VW in Santa Clara, California. Nancy is in foreground. *Below:* Steve, second from right, at age eleven with neighborhood friends.

On the gridiron in 1979.

Steve and his wife, Sandee, at their wedding, January 1980.

Steve, in center, in 1978 against the New York Giants.

Steve in 1977 against the San Francisco 49ers.

Author Dan DeHaan, left, with Steve in 1980 during final consultation for this book.

6

Disappointments or His Appointments

The Bible is a book of tragedies. It seems that the Lord chose to record every kind of calamity in His Word. He could have hidden some of the terrible events which His children would experience, but He chose to reveal them. The lessons we have learned from Him are worth every bit of the struggle we must go through.

To teach these disappointments to a new Christian is an interesting struggle in itself. In the early days of Steve's conversion, I wanted him to know that when he had nothing left but God, then for the first time he would learn that God Himself was enough. God's glory is at stake even in our difficulties and disappointments. He will not share His glory with another (Isaiah 42:8). The most outrageous moment for the devil will be when he finds that in spite of himself, he has done everything according to God's permissive will. The same is true of the man who has been serving his own self.

Sometime ago, Steve said, "Dan, I can't understand why God would let me fail the way I did today on the field." He had played a good game, but was deeply concerned about "chewing out" a teammate for running a wrong pass pattern.

He continued, "God knows I want to live for Him in all I do. Why would He allow me to blow my top like that?"

Another time he questioned me about the goodness of God in relation to so many tragic events among Christians. "How do we explain these things?" he asked.

My answers might be simple, but I believe they are scriptural and serve to illustrate some biblical principles. This chapter is devoted to helping us see God's view when many adverse situations come our way.

When difficulties occur in our life, we may adopt a wrong view of God. Let me illustrate. If you were to take a perfectly straight stick and put it into the water, it would appear to be crooked. Why? Because we look at it through two mediums: air and water. Some people may see God's justice, for example, as crooked. They see the wicked prosper while the righteous suffer. They see Israel making bricks to house the evil Egyptians. Many similar unfair events seem to take place. It appears so because we look upon God's proceedings through a double medium: Flesh and Spirit. Therefore, it is not God's character which is bent, it is the eyes of men who are not competent to judge.

God knows everything! (Psalms 147:5). He also has the power to change anything (Psalms 115:3). In order to adequately understand God, we must begin at this point. If God has an infinite amount of knowledge and wisdom, we must never say that God made a mistake. It is better to say that we don't know very much! Our limitations are too limited to question One with no limitations. There is simply too much that we do not know. Even what we do know has been revealed to us by God Himself. Without Him, we would know nothing!

God is not a celestial chess player, awaiting the unknown move, and then making a counter move. God is sovereign! He does what He likes and He always acts in wisdom (Romans 16:27). Those who are called liberals, in their view of the Bible, may be well meaning when they attempt to show God as having nothing to do with the evil of this world. But they deprive God of being in control. It is important to realize that the glory of God is the ultimate end of all His actions. Our happiness is not that end. God's glory is!

Steve battled with these thoughts before he committed his life to Christ. "If I give my life to Christ, what will I have to give up?" he asked himself. Several players on the Falcons, as well as many sincere people around the world, have the same question in their minds. The important point to remember is that God is never looking for a person to sacrifice as an end in itself. You see, nobody gives up so much as those who are most determined to give up nothing!

When the Prodigal Son of Luke 15 went into the far country, he certainly had no thought of making any sacrifice. But in spite of this fact, he found the adventure to be very costly. It cost him the companionship of his father. It cost him gnawing hungers and burning thirsts. It cost him his usefulness. In fact, it cost him everything—he literally spent all that he had. It remains true, therefore, that none surrender so much as those who are most determined to surrender nothing.

Steve had to learn, as all of us must, that God wants to use us to vindicate His character to the world. The preface to Job's story sheds light on this point of view. God's honor was at stake in the issue fought out in Job's soul. God's honor was vindicated in Job's life.

Notice the lives of men who have been used mightily by God. Every one of them had to face the loss of friendships, loss of possessions, or the loss of their worldly greatness. God did not say that we will lose if we follow Him, but He did say that we must count the cost of losing should we decide to choose Him. Those of us who have decided to follow Him would never turn back. Any man in his right mind would not turn back. The gain is too glorious to cry about the loss!

After we have been through the superficial experiences of life, we will find that we are built with a greater capacity for pain than for joy. God's choice expression for the world is the cross, not joy. When we align ourselves with God, we begin to think differently about sacrifice. Before his conversion, Steve believed that he would rather get what he could now, even if he had to pay for it later. Since he became a Christian, he says, "I would rather sacrifice now and get what God has for me later."

No one in his right mind would want to deal with God's divine lay-away plan: "Sin now, pay later!" (*see* 2 Corinthians 4:16–18).

After signing his autograph, Steve now writes the Scripture reference for the verse which has become his life's theme— Galatians 2:20. In this verse we find the pain of being crucified with Christ. While it may not mean physical pain to the average Christian, it will cost him to become one with Christ. He will suffer rejection as Christ suffered rejection. He will have to give up the same rights that Christ gave. He must die for those things for which Christ died and live for those things for which Christ lives. This is what it means!

God will usually take a person and allow a series of disappointments to come his way, with the purpose of letting him see God's appointments through them. The longer it takes him to see God in the valley, the longer he will be in the valley's darkness. Many times we find ourselves insisting to be free from the surrounding difficulties. When we do, we have not yet learned of God in that difficulty, or we have failed to unlearn some of our former ways. When we learn to see events as His appointments, then we can go through any trial and God's character will not be marred through our lives.

If there were no clouds in our lives, we would not need the sustaining faith that God wants to teach us. For those separated from God, clouds and difficulties are accidents. But, by those same clouds, the Spirit of God teaches us to walk by faith. Steve's life verse also states that his desire is to walk according to the faith of the Son of God. This means that Steve Bartkowski will have to experience more clouds in his life than he has already. God loves to reveal Himself in clouds. We can easily see Him in the clearing, but what a surprise to find Him in the clouds also.

It may not be true that God wants us to learn something in our trials. Quite often, He may want us to *unlearn* something. He wants us to simplify our belief in Him until our relationship to Him is childlike. However, God will use every cloud in our lives to bring us nearer to Himself. He wants us to know what it is to experience untroubled hearts as His is.

"According to what I have heard," Steve told me, "Christianity will probably add to my difficulties."

"No, Steve," I answered. "Christianity does not add to our difficulties. It brings them into focus, so in the midst of them, we find Jesus Christ. It thrills God to see us struggling through difficulties, and all of a sudden, we find Him there helping us. What an oasis!"

Like so many of us, God wants Steve to unlearn many things. We should all ask ourselves the question "What do I know that God doesn't want me to know? How must I go about unlearning those things?" The Bible teaches us that God will do it through the pruning process. He will cut back in order to give you a more beautiful bloom. It is also true that God sends us clouds in order to make other people less influential in our lives (John 15).

One day Steve came to me with an interesting complaint. "I'm finding my devotions a bit dry lately. What's wrong with me?"

"Probably nothing," I answered. "You see, God may be wanting to take a habit, such as devotions, and turn it into a reality. He may be wanting you to see that you cannot trust in your devotions to keep you straight. Only God can do that!"

God may be wanting us to get acquainted with a new method of devotions or study. He sends us clouds to help us unlearn something old and to learn something new in its place. We should never make a move while we are in the valley of clouds. We must learn to wait! Let Him pull us out. *Our feeble attempt to crawl out will cause us to miss His appointments.*

God's goal for each of us is to be able to look full in the face at the blackest disappointment and come out of it without damaging His character. There is no such thing as calamities or accidents to God's children. ". . . all things work together for good . . ." (Romans 8:28). Sin and evil, or for that matter, the devil himself, cannot catch God by surprise. "This is my

Father's world, and let us never forget; that though the wrong seems, oh, so strong, God is the ruler yet."

The cross of Christ pronounced final and irrevocable judgment against the prince of this world (John 12:31). When Steve Bartkowski was crucified with Christ, the devil couldn't do a thing about it. All he can do now is scare Steve into thinking that it didn't happen. God knows that Steve's defense will demand a strong faith. Therefore, God sends trials and difficulties to strengthen his faith.

During the first year of Bible study with the Falcon players and their wives, I emphasized a specific verse in the Book of James, chapter 1, on counting it all joy when you fall into various trials and testings. This passage shows us *God's purposes for the difficulties we go through.* The following list is certainly not all inclusive, but the points are worth mentioning.

1. JOY. The knowledge that God is making Himself known to you through a difficulty should produce joy.

2. ENDURANCE. The Christian life is a marathon run, not a hundred-yard dash. Trials make us strong. Nobody ever sharpens his knife on a stick of butter. We will not sharpen our lives through easy times, either. It takes going against the grain.

3. COMPLETENESS IN CHARACTER. One sure way God makes the Christian life balanced is through trials. We are prone to get cocky and self-assured without trials.

4. WISDOM. God supplies wisdom as we get desperate for it. Our desperation comes only through trials.

5. FAITH. This grows best in unfavorable soil. Everything else is just religious jargon until real faith is experienced.

6. STABILITY. God uses trials to keep us from wandering from those things which He wants to teach us.

God also gives us a sixfold curriculum to study and learn while we are experiencing trials. The six are found in James

1:19–22. When you are experiencing difficulties, make a special effort to practice these six priorities.

1. BE QUICK TO HEAR. Listen very carefully to God's people and to the Lord Himself. God is wanting to reveal Himself to you. Stay in the Word of God!

2. BE SLOW TO SPEAK. Quit talking as much as possible, when you are going through great difficulties. You will miss what God is wanting to say. You are also apt to say the wrong things when you are under great pressure.

3. BE SLOW TO ANGER. Realize that this is a time in your life when you are confused and can get unusually frustrated. Consciously lay down your right to anger.

4. PUT ASIDE ALL FILTHINESS. When you are going through times of difficulty, get a sheet of paper and write down any personal errors that could have contributed to the trial. If these are people you should confess to, then do it! If there is a personal cleansing God wants you to express, then do it.

5. IN HUMILITY, RECEIVE THE WORD. This addition to the list suggests that the person stay quiet when he is under trials and testings. Stay in the Word and stay out of the world. With the attitude of a needy child, read the Word of God.

6. PROVE YOURSELF TO BE A DOER OF THE WORD AND NOT MERELY A HEARER. When trials abound, minister to others. The problem with so many who are in difficult trials is that they keep asking themselves, "Why is this happening to me?" God desires that we reach out to those in need, even when we ourselves are in great need.

Perhaps you can see why James 1:27 is given at this particular time. During unusual times of difficulty, it tells us to go minister to orphans and widows. We always consider ourselves unfortunate until we see others who are less fortunate than we are.

There was once a man who found a cocoon on a tree in his yard. He was intrigued by it and decided to watch it change. One day, he saw a tiny butterfly inside the delicate covering and he watched it struggling, trying its best to break out of its captivity. Finally, the man became so frustrated that he decided to use a razor blade to make a tiny slit in the side of the cocoon, in order to free the struggling butterfly. Soon afterward, the butterfly was free, but it could not fly and finally died prematurely. ONLY IN STRUGGLES DO WE OBTAIN STRENGTH.

An eagle has a unique wing formation, so that according to the laws of aerodynamics, he cannot fly. Men today are still baffled as to how the eagle can fly. Yet, it is known as the strongest and most free-flying bird in the universe. It is important to notice how the mother eagle teaches her young to fly. She carries the young one on her back, high above the trees, often on top of the highest mountain. While soaring at a high altitude, she throws the young bird off of her back and watches it plummet toward the ground. In panic, the untrained eaglet flaps its wings to no avail. After all, the eagle, by all physical standards, is not supposed to be able to fly. Yet the mother eagle continues the trying experience of teaching her young to fly. It goes on and on until the young bird can soar on its own, but not until it faces near death does the mother eagle swoop down to save the falling young one. Remember, ONLY IN THE STRUGGLE DO WE OBTAIN THE STRENGTH. God has had to let His children fall many times, only to catch us at the last moment. However, lessons learned and the strength gained are worth the trials.

7

I'm a Saint

Before Steve was ready to share his Christian testimony in public, I wanted him to grasp the most important truth of the Scriptures. That truth is our position in Christ! He was somewhat surprised when I was less than enthusiastic about his making personal appearances to share his testimony. While it was true that God could use Steve's story in a great way, it is equally true that the power of God in a testimony does not demand a superhero, or some former "Satan follower" to gain attention.

While each of us should be ready to give our testimony when called upon, God does not use just those who have previously been "hooked" by Satan in some way. Several people have said, "Sometimes I wish I had been involved in some evil lifestyle before my conversion. Maybe some Christian program would think I was important enough to ask me to give my testimony." We must remember, God is not looking for someone bad enough to share his testimony, but He is looking for those who are "mature" enough to be able to endure with His power. His goodness, which He transplants in man, takes time for growth. Because of the growing process, I constantly tried to hold Steve back from "hitting the road" for Jesus. Before sharing his testimony publicly, he must first learn about his position in Christ.

I will never forget the liberating expression and the joyous words Steve shared with me when he first embraced the truth of his position in Christ. Nothing had a bigger impact on his life, and his desire for this book was that others might experience the same truth.

In one of our continuing discussions, I told Steve the major problem of many Christians is their unbiblical view of Christianity. They have a tendency to look at the new life in terms of what it forbids. They think about what they must separate themselves from, rather than taking the approach of the Apostle Paul and thinking about what they are separated *unto.* In their opinion, Christianity is more repression than expression. It supplies weights rather than wings!

It was in this message that I saw Steve Bartkowski freed from several areas of his past and present life. It gave him freedom from spiritual intimidation. After realizing his position in Christ, he was free to be himself. He did not have to spend his time trying to be like other Christians who were more spiritual. It also gave him freedom from guilt, as well as freedom from fear. He began to have an unusual confidence that God was in control. The key word for Steve's new understanding of his position in Christ was *freedom.*

Using Romans chapter 6 and Colossians chapter 2, Steve became well grounded in this principle. I had not realized the tremendous impact this truth would make upon his life. He had spent months trying to pull himself out of his drifting pattern, but all his fleshly attempts failed.

One Tuesday evening, while having dessert at a restaurant in Atlanta, I sat across from the struggling, broken quarterback for the Falcons.

"I know I should be doing better," Steve told me dejectedly. "I just don't know what is wrong. I really want to serve the Lord and be His man."

I knew then that he was struggling for spiritual growth. I prayed that God would free him to enjoy the Christian life, unfettered by all the demands of his peers.

Steve and his fiancée, Sandee Oliver, began attending the Metro Bible Study in Atlanta, where I was teaching on Colossians 2 and Romans 6. During the latter part of the summer, before the football season began, Sandee had been trying to encourage Steve to grasp the principle of his position in Christ. During the study, Steve literally "leaped for joy" as he began to understand the greatness of his position as a Christian.

"You just have to share this with all the Falcons in our Bible study this fall," he demanded. His insistence, coupled with the new joy I saw in his life, convinced me that his teammates and their wives could benefit from such a study. I am also convinced that many "mature" Christians could benefit from the study. For that reason, I am including many of its main points.

Colossians chapter 2 is loaded with biblical doctrine. In the passage between verses 9 and 15, we are given a list of God's views as to who we are in Christ Jesus. Once we hear God's testimony about ourselves, we will never listen to foreign voices again.

"And in Him you have been made complete. . . ." This is the key to our position in Christ, and it means that a person in Him has no less than He has. We have become full; there is no way to add to it. It is finished! All rulers, principalities, and powers have nothing to add to His work. Christ is the completer. He does nothing halfway. Whatever He touched in the Gospels became whole.

When it comes to explaining our position in Christ in Colossians chapter 2, He continues this completeness in us. It is here that we see three important descriptions: 1) Complete salvation, verses 11, 12, and 2) Complete forgiveness, verses 13, 14, and 3) Complete victory, verse 15.

For the first time, Steve could see his salvation as COMPLETE. The depth of the Christian experience is only realized to the degree we understand this truth. The moment a person is in Christ, he is in a position of fullness. It is an accomplished fact! One hundred thirty times within his thirteen letters Paul emphasized his high position in Christ.

Your position in Christ does not change. It is like a baby when it is born. He is given a complete body with all its parts.

There is no grafting of an eye after birth, or an ear three days later, or a nose two weeks after it is born. The baby has all of its normal parts when it is born. The only thing it lacks is growth—the strengthening of the given parts. The same is true of married persons. They can't be more married. They are either married or they are not married!

". . . and He is the head over all rule and authority." This tells us that the completeness of our salvation cannot be overthrown by someone's new law or even the devil's authority. God pronounced us complete and no one can change that fact! Verse 11 continues to explain the same context that in Him we were also circumcised without hands. This exercise proved that it was human nature that had to be dealt with, the passing of sin from father to son. The very context of circumcision implies that it is nature being dealt with, not just putting away certain sins.

Do you believe that when Steve became a Christian, God took away his old nature? Absolutely yes! It happened to Steve as well as to me, and if you are in Christ, it happened to you. We were circumcised from the old nature. It was cut away, removed, cast aside from us. Yet Steve would ask, "Well, if my old nature is done away with, why do I still sin?" The answer is that we have a new nature within an old body.

Romans chapter 7 reinforces the power of this doctrinal passage. Verses 17 and 18 tell us that Paul was hassled with the old body, but his new nature had replaced the old. "No longer am *I* the one doing it, but sin which indwells me. For I know that nothing good dwells in me, that is, *in my flesh* . . ." (my italics). Verse 22 tells us that our new nature truly loves God. It wants to serve the Lord, respond to Him, and do every good thing. But sin is in our members (verse 23). The old nature within me has been created anew; but the body is a mess! You see, when we get to heaven, we are not going to get a new nature. It is not even implied that we will lose the old one. But it is stated quite clearly that we will get a new body. Why? It is the only thing hindering practical perfection. Paul climaxes the chapter by saying, ". . . with my mind I serve the law of God, but my flesh serves sin" (*see* verse 25).

When Steve became a Christian, he did not get "whitewashed." He became brand-new! His new nature is still surrounded by the old flesh, which has been used to sinning for a long time. It will still rebel against righteousness. Sin has been passed on through Adam, but the last Adam, Jesus Christ, dealt with it completely. The covenant promises throughout the Bible that God will give us a new heart. Romans 8 is the message of Paul, bringing the flesh into harmony with his new nature, through walking in the Spirit.

Colossians chapter 2 continues to emphasize this complete salvation through verse 13. Notice the past tense, actually the aorist tense, of the verbs. "Having been buried . . . you were also raised up. . . ." Here Paul is picturing the union of a believer with Christ. We have been placed into Christ. This is baptism! Faith buries a man. It slams the man on the cross, it buries him with Christ, and it resurrects the man with Christ. Every Christian becomes intimately identified with Christ. This was all done through the energies of God.

Look at Romans 6:6. Does it say that our old nature was crucified with Him, that our body of sin might be slightly altered? No! It says, ". . . that our body of sin might be done away with. . . ." It is destroyed! This does not mean we are free from ever doing it again, but it does mean we are free from its consequences and desire. The Bible says, "the wages of sin is death" (Romans 6:23). But how many times can sin kill a man? Only once! If you are a Christian, you have already died. We died once and it's the devil's own tough luck that we rose from the dead! Sin has no claim on us. Since it is true that the wages of sin is death, every man must die for his sin—either alone or in Christ. The reason physical death is a joy for the Christian is that to him it means just getting rid of the perplexing problem, the body. Terrific! Free from sin's bondage. He died once and we died with Him. Now, when Satan comes to bug you about how imperfect you are, just tell him to get off your back and go bug someone who doesn't know their Bible, especially their position in Christ.

Next, let us notice the COMPLETE FORGIVENESS we have. Colossians 2:13 and 14 gives us the doctrinal input necessary for this study. It speaks of having been forgiven of "all our transgressions." ALL must mean just that! This verse tells us again that our forgiveness is apart from works. "He made you alive." "You were dead." These phrases show us our inability to respond. The phrase "dead in your sins" is in the case called "locative of position." It literally means "born dead with an inability to respond." The Bible teaches us that we cannot respond to God apart from His first working in us.

We have all heard the phrase "I found the Lord." I know what it implies, but it is incorrect. The truth is that the Lord found you. He was never lost, you were. He was never dead, you were. The first major benefit to this awakening is that we have ALL OUR TRANSGRESSIONS FORGIVEN (Psalms 32:1; Isaiah 55:7; Acts 13:38).

Many Christians continue to remember what God has forgotten. The highest court in the universe is God. If God has forgiven you, and you do not believe it, then you must think you are higher than God. Yet, these are the very thoughts of many people. God's forgiveness is complete! In Psalms 103:12, the Bible says, "As far as the east is from the west,/So far has/ He removed our transgressions from us." This teaches us that there is no such thing as an unforgiven sin in the life of a Christian. You may ask, why ask forgiveness then? Because asking forgiveness restores our joy in the Lord and it puts us in a position to receive from the Lord.

Notice the phrase, "Having cancelled out the certificate of debt" (Colossians 2:14). In Paul's day, this was literally a handwritten debt. It was a signed confession of debt. This phrase tells us that our sins piled up a debt to God against us and He erased the certificate of debt, took it out of the way. Also notice, "Having nailed it to the cross." Now, when the devil accuses you, take him to the cross and ask him what he has to say against Christ. Christ's complete perfections have been given to you.

Finally, in this passage Paul talks about our COMPLETE VICTORY in Christ. "When He had disarmed the rulers and authorities, He made a public display of them, having triumphed over them through Him" (verse 15). The phrase "having triumphed over" is a phrase to depict a wrestling match. If you have ever observed tag-team wrestling, then you can quickly identify this picture. If an opponent has your friend pinned to the floor and is abusing him, you know that before you can come into the ring to render assistance, you must touch your partner's hand. When that is done, you jump over the ropes and take the opponent off your partner and beat him soundly. Well, this is what Jesus did for us! We were pinned by the devil himself. He had us down and we were helpless and hopeless in our condition. With one touch of the nail-scarred hand of Jesus, He came in and threw off with ease our opponent, the devil. Since that time, Satan has been made a fool in every Christian's life. Experientially, he is the fool every time we put our total faith and trust in the complete victory that Christ has so freely offered us.

If someone were to pay off your personal debt of several thousand dollars, then gave you all of their own personal possessions and, in addition, gave you their love like no one had ever done before, what would be your response to him? I am sure it would be a response of gratitude and love. You would immediately say, "What can I do for you?" "Can I help you in anyway whatsoever?" "Thank you, thank you, thank you!" It is this response that delights God most. He is looking for children who love Him and are thankful to Him. Remember, though, we will be judged according to the motives we had for serving the Lord. There can be no higher motive than love for serving Him.

At the conclusion of this study, Steve Bartkowski's life took on new meaning. I trust that God will always keep this truth before him and that Steve's response will always be, "What can I do for You, Lord?" How about you? Are you sure you are "in" Christ? Do you understand what your position in Him means? Are you expressing true love and gratitude for such an eternal gift?

8

Secure and Sensitive in Marriage

Someone has said that man has a heart that is incurably romantic. God made each of us with this distinct characteristic and He desires to see us enjoy this gift. God knew that after an unsuccessful marriage, Steve needed someone to share his life and fill that romantic vacuum in his heart.

Shortly after his conversion, you remember that Steve spent the off-season at his parents' home in California. It was during this time that he began drifting away from fellowship with other Christians and an intimate walk with the Lord. His best friend, Mike Hodgins, who had joined him in Atlanta to ease his loneliness, experienced an unfortunate accident when he fell from a scaffold and broke his back. Steve became quite depressed, and seeing his best friend paralyzed for life added to his dilemma. The lack of Christian fellowship caused Steve to make some wrong decisions in his life. He dated girls who were suggested by well-meaning friends, but many were insecure and not what he expected or was seeking. After each date, he felt the same loneliness as before.

God knew what was happening to Steve. He was not about to let him go. The young Christian was in no condition to seek friendships at a Bible study, yet God knew that Steve was in desperate need of having friendship sent from heaven. This is when He sent Sandee Oliver into the picture.

Steve first met Sandee in February 1979, while playing racquetball in North Atlanta. She is a beautiful, active girl, with large brown eyes and brown, flowing hair. Fun loving and a joy to be around, she is also the epitome of a girl who has found real freedom in Christ. I have known Sandee for several years and have admired her deep security in her Christian life. This same security baffled Steve for some time before their marriage.

Sandee, the youngest of three sisters, became a Christian when she was fourteen years old. She spent some time modeling before managing an investment office in Atlanta, the job she held when she met Steve. Her best friend, Pam Housley, married Pat Terry, the lead singer for the Pat Terry Group. After Pam's marriage, Sandee felt very lonely and believed that marriage for her might never be, or at least was a long way off. She dated several fellows, but none were interesting enough for her to think of marriage. She learned to put the situation in the hands of the Lord and believed that if He wanted her to be married someday, He would bring about the circumstances and the person in His will. She was encouraged to see the beautiful relationship between Pam and Pat, two wonderful Christians who put Christ first in their marriage.

"When I met Sandee, it was like a calm after the storm," Steve said. "I was already too tired to fight in the Christian life. I'd had too many defeats in a row and out of disgust for my lazy walk with God, was ready to quit. The first night we were out after a Bible-study meeting, I shared with Sandee my continuing struggles. She was really a rock for me. God only knows the needs I had."

When Sandee told me that she had met Steve and they were dating, I was elated. I had prayed for Steve during his struggle and now I was beginning to see my prayers partially answered. Actually, until Sandee came into Steve's life, I had seen less and less of him. It seemed that he was purposely avoiding fellowship with other Christians. But God was using Sandee to pull him out of his drifting pattern. Steve was looking for a Christian girl. All the while God knew that he would meet

Sandee, marry her, and that she would be the means of teaching him security and sensitivity in marriage.

"I don't know why I insisted on going back to California," Steve said. "I suppose the devil just made going back very attractive. But Sandee came into my life and really pulled me out of the depths of despair."

In May and June of that year, Steve and Sandee began attending the Metro Bible Study regularly. This is a Bible study of several hundred people that meets every Tuesday evening in Atlanta. We would get together after the meetings on several occasions for dessert and a chance to chat. I was thrilled to see that God was beginning to work closely in their lives. I was teaching Romans 6 during this time and Steve became so enthusiastic that he rode the waves of its impact for several weeks. Sandee continued to be a stabilizing influence in his life, without showing any signs of having a permanent relationship in mind.

Because of his position as quarterback of the Falcons and his prominence in Atlanta circles, many girls were interested in dating Steve. Yet he seemed to have an innate ability to tell if a girl was pushing herself upon him. Sandee kept Steve guessing about their relationship for a long time. She seemed to be so secure without him that Steve really wondered if she needed him the way he needed her.

One day after practice, Steve said, "The thing that makes Sandee so special is that she seems so content without me. She seems to really know her place and never tries to make me feel like I have to be a certain way to please her."

"How are you two doing?" I inquired of Steve.

"Well," Steve hesitated. "We have started to talk quite seriously."

"Did you ask her to marry you?"

Steve did not reply for a moment, then said, "Yes, I asked her and she said that I was not ready for that yet. Personally, I became a bit angry with her."

I encouraged Steve to continue some serious talks with her. A few months and a few serious talks later, Steve asked her again if she would marry him, and Sandee accepted the proposal.

"I wanted to accept his proposal from the very beginning," Sandee said. "But I knew marriage was a serious step. I did not want my emotions running ahead of His will. I loved Steve, but I wanted to be very sure he was serious before my commitment came."

In October 1979, they became engaged and decided that they would be married in April, after the completion of the football season. However, they moved the date to January 19, immediately after the football season closed. I had the pleasure, along with my good friend Ron Braund, to marry Sandee and Steve. It was indeed a joy!

The wedding was very casual, and personally, I wish all weddings were the same. While they stood together before their marriage altar, I subconsciously reviewed what God had done for them. I felt like a proud father, who would bring the last and best presents to his children on Christmas morning. The wedding was very sacred; yet the seriousness and superiority of marriage was a great thrill to them.

During the ceremony, Steve and Sandee were both so conscious of what was being said. They listened to every word spoken to them. They were agreeing to share their lives together, while at the same time, they understood their freedom as individuals and respected each other's right to be themselves.

"I was afraid of losing my identity," Sandee confessed, "because I now was Steve's wife instead of Sandee Oliver. Then I realized that my personhood was the very thing that would make me minister to Steve the most."

It is true that many people marry because of a role they expect the other one to fill. They want to change the other's personality and begin to demand certain things of their spouse that are either impossible or make the other feel very uncomfortable. Sandee said, "I believe that communication is the key to our marriage. If I feel that something is not in order, I am tempted, because of my personality, to remain quiet. However, I have learned the importance of talking to Steve about any problem and issue, and have already seen the value of communication."

"Marriage is not tough," Steve said recently. "If you both love the Lord and have that common denominator, marriage can be easy. When you get right back to your main purpose as Christians to glorify God, it demands that you get things right with one another when they are wrong."

There are many couples who are unhappily married. Some resent seeing others who enjoy their marital bliss, and the Bartkowskis have sensed some resentment from unhappy couples, because they seem to be so happily married. The key to Steve and Sandee's happiness has been Christ as their foundation, openness in their communication, and sensitivity in their relationship to one another.

"If these areas are present in your life," Steve believes, "then marriage is easy."

Prior to their marriage, I gave Steve and Sandee a book entitled *Magnificent Marriage* by Gordon McDonald. I consider this book one of the best on the subject of marriage. While studying this book, the Bartkowskis became aware of the need for being sensitive to each other's needs and desires. Steve admitted, "To look at each situation from the other's point of view was a needed lesson for me." Sandee voiced the same opinion. Many married couples seem to forget that they are to be sensitive to each other's needs.

Sensitivity produces positive unity and oneness between two people. It also keeps romance alive! Ridicule and sarcasm may be fun at times, but few people know when to stop. This jesting, even in fun, can kill romance. Even to call a partner's thoughts an "absurd idea" or to offer sincere affection to your spouse and be cut off can damage a marriage quickly.

Suppose a happy husband comes into his house and exclaims, "Honey, I wish I could take a trip around the world with you!" How would you respond? If you are sensitive to your husband, you would probably say, "Well, that would be great. I would love it, too, but I don't think we can afford it right now. Maybe someday." On the other hand, if you are not sensitive to your husband, you might say, "You know we don't have the money for a trip like that. Why do you always talk about such expensive things?" The husband knows the money is not available. He is not even suggesting that you pack the bags for the trip. He is reaching out to his wife, wanting to dream about something nice together. If he is cut off, it may be a long time before he shares another dream with his wife.

Being sensitive also means being willing to express yourself often. Thank you's should be shared several times every day between people in the same house. It means that you avoid being hyperserious most of the time, when you color every situation gray. It means that you are content to love your spouse and let God change him or her if there is a need. One woman prayed, "Lord, you love him and I will change him." What a tragic mistake.

There are other weapons which many couples use that kill their sensitivity and romance. Silence is one of the most deadly ones used by many people. While many Christians would never use profanity, yet they will evoke the most profane silence in the world.

The use of word missiles can also kill romance. These nonsensitive words and phrases can destroy relationships. For instance, "I'm sick and tired of your constant . . ." or "I'm never going to satisfy you. . . ." These are known as verbal overkills. We use these strong statements to gain control of the conversation when we see we are losing the battle. This is when we need to forget our own rights and confess our insensitivity.

Consider the differences among the following statements: 1. "I see your point." 2. "Okay, if it will make you happy." 3. "You always come up with dumb ideas like this." The first statement will keep you and your spouse together. The second is implying that your partner is very hard to please. The third is dropping a verbal atomic bomb. It is slandering your marriage partner.

"The choicest way to bring out the best in one another is to serve each other." In doing so, we surrender our own personal rights in preference to the other, which makes the love increase in marriage. To expect to receive from the other, while not being willing to give, will only add to frustration and deterioration in a relationship.

"Security in marriage is one of the greatest things in the world," Steve says. "Sandee and I find our security in Christ first and in our sensitivity to one another as we live our lives together." Secure marriages are that way because two people have found security in their relationship with Christ before seeking it in one another.

9

Getting to Know God

Have you ever noticed that many people today like to brag about things they possess or have accomplished on their own? The Bible is very specific concerning bragging about any earthly thing, even the self-assurance of having another day to live. Most people like to talk about themselves or their own interests. Many of them are like the little newsboy who was asked why he sold newspapers when he only made two cents on each sale. "It gives me a chance to holler!" he replied.

There are some today who will espouse any cause that affords them a chance to "holler." But God said, "Let not a wise man boast of his wisdom, and let not the mighty man boast of his might, let not a rich man boast of his riches; but let him who boasts boast of this, *that he understands and knows Me* . . ." (Jeremiah 9:23,24 my italics).

One of the recent lessons Steve Bartkowski has learned has been about bragging. God has taught him to brag and be proud of only one thing: that is the knowledge he has of Jesus Christ.

"It bothers me to see Christians who are not proud to be sons of God," he said. "There is nothing like it in the whole world and no greater attainment than to know God." This was no slight remark, because he has said this to me several times in our conversations.

"Paul said that he counted all things as loss for the knowledge of Christ," Steve added. "Nothing compares to it in all the world." If you are a Christian who is not pursuing the knowledge of Christ as your number-one goal, you are missing a great truth. There can be no higher calling or motivation in life.

We are aware of the fact that there are many people who say they do not believe in God. If you should ever share your faith with such a person, you should ask him if he has been everywhere in this great universe. If he says yes, you may have a problem on your hands. But, you know he must admit that he has not. A person cannot be a legitimate atheist because he has not been everywhere to prove that God does not exist. He may be an agnostic and say, "I don't think there is a God." You might tell him that the Latin word for agnostic is *ignoramus.* You might want to pause momentarily before you call him such an adverse name. But if a person believes there is a God, you have made a significant beginning.

God has revealed Himself to us throughout the Bible. He is not provable in an empirical sense, because unlike other objects of science, He is above the laws of investigation. In fact, He invented the very laws with which He would be investigated. In Psalm 14, there is a very penetrating verse: "The fool has said in his heart, 'There is no God' " (verse 1). Why should any person be an atheist? This verse answers the question! The Hebrew word for "fool" means "the vicious, wicked one." He is a fool because he has deceived himself into believing that God will not require punishment for his sin. However, if he does believe in God, then he knows he will have to stop his "vicious wickedness." When we try to deceive ourselves, God calls this "foolishness."

God is a fact, and being deceived and denying it does not change the fact. A practical atheist may believe that "pleasure is the highest good." This may sound good to the pragmatic person, but when a person dies, what then?

An atheist may say that "you Christians live by faith." And he is right. We do live by faith in the Creator of all things. Can you imagine that everything in this universe was created by no one? I believe in God because of the law of cause and effect. If I were to take you to my house and tell you that it is the result of an explosion in a lumber yard, you would probably call me an idiot! You know that the first cause had to have intelligence. God: He is, and He has revealed Himself to those who seek Him. Therefore, there is nothing greater to brag about than that God has been revealed to you.

The renowned Francis Schaeffer said recently, "We live in an age of mad selfishness." Really, we are reaping the results of several generations of worshiping ourselves. We live by the philosophy of "grab all the gusto you can find, even if it hurts the one next to you!" It is the self-enthroned egotist who destroys what he touches. But it is the self-dethroned man who has the joy of watching God restore all the years that self-destruction has taken. The Christian has learned to believe in one big, bold miracle—GOD! And everything else falls in place. An atheist denies God and must have a miracle for every other thing created.

God's purpose for His most prized creation, man, was that we would bring Him glory. This was the reason we were created. As Steve continued to grow in his Christian life, he said, "My purpose in life is to glorify God now. I must admit that before I became a Christian, my purpose was to lift up Steve and his concerns."

When God saves a man, He lets him know that his salvation was not just for himself, but it was primarily for God. God loves to reveal Himself to us in order to let us appreciate who He is and therefore become more like Him. Most fathers delight in seeing their children becoming more like them. As God is perfect in all His ways, He also delights in our understanding and knowledge of who He is. As we worship Him we become like Him!

It is evident that many Christians have a poor view of their heavenly Father and it shows in their daily walk. They have been saved, but they have stopped pursuing God! They grow frustrated because they are trying to live a life like Christ and do not know Him well enough. Remember, the Apostle Paul's entire goal in life is summarized in the words of Philippians

3:10: "I [want] to know Him." And he wrote that after he had known the Lord for more than thirty years. He was speaking of knowing God intimately. He knew the difference between a superficial knowledge of God and KNOWING Him. One is a quick prayer, while the other demands discipline and intensive pursuing.

One of the beautiful things about knowing God and being comfortable in our relationship with Him is that other foreign voices seem to fade away. We all need to learn the art of "not paying attention to the other voices." Jesus paid no attention to what many said about Him. There were those who told Him that the sword was the way to power. He paid no attention to them. There were those who warned Him earnestly against the cross. He paid no attention to them. Still others said that the way to win was to be a go-getter. He still paid no attention. He knew God intimately and came to do His will. All foreign voices went unheeded.

Steve had to learn this lesson and I was thrilled at his progress. He said, "I used to be so conscious of what was being written about me. Now, I hardly read a paper. I used to be so aware of what the public thinks, but now I know that only one person matters in my life and thoughts. That Person is Jesus Christ!"

It takes time to know God well. Steve is still learning some of this continuing lesson. God desires to teach him, and he wants to know God above all other things. God will separate him for private lessons. It will be a painful experience at times for anyone who wants to know God better, but He will teach him out of that experience to know His voice better and to pay less attention to other voices.

When we have a knowledge of God, we will be more intense in our service to Him. Many Christians serve the Lord out of performance or practice, but have very little passion. You may learn performance at school, but only God can give you passion. You can learn to witness in a seminar, but only God can make you weep over lost souls. You may even learn to pray by listening to friends, but only God can teach you to "pour yourself out before Him."

We must not become halfhearted in our search to know God. To be halfhearted is to fail. Suppose you were challenged to take a giant leap across a river. After you had accepted the challenge, you realized that you might fail, but friends encouraged you to go ahead. Just as you were about to make the giant leap, someone cried, "Stop, stop, stop!" and instead of closing out the negative voice, you listened enough to jump only halfheartedly. You would probably land right in the middle of the river. Remember what James said in chapter 1, verse 8? "Being a double-minded man, unstable in all his ways."

The world will rob us of our intensity and replace it with a halfhearted attitude in all we do. We must learn the art of not paying attention to the world—to close out foreign voices. The knowledge of God is the answer. Get to know Him well!

How can the average Christian avoid paying attention to all the foreign voices we hear? The best way is to tune out the worthless and to tune in the worthful. In the Old Testament, we repeatedly read that "God said." We also read that "the serpent said." While it is true that God is still broadcasting, so is the serpent. But it is our high privilege to tune in on God and know His voice, and as a result, we will hush those lower voices into silence. This has been the way of the saints through all the centuries.

> Faith, mighty faith, the promise sees,
>   and looks to God alone;
> Laughs at impossibilities,
>   and cries, "It shall be done."

Knowing that God is UNCHANGEABLE (Psalms 102:26, 27), comforts me in the fact that if He forgave me before, He will forgive me now! If He loved me before, He loves me now.

Knowing that God is EVERYWHERE (Jeremiah 23:23,24), comforts me when I read, "I will never leave you or forsake you." It also convinces me that "all my ways are before Him." He sees it all! No sin, motive, or attitude is hidden from Him.

Knowing that God is ALL POWERFUL (Psalms 115:3) is a comfort to my inadequacy!

Knowing that God KNOWS EVERYTHING (Psalms 147:5) is a comfort to me in that He knows and meets my needs.

Knowing God's HOLINESS (Exodus 15:11) makes me rejoice that it has been given to me now.

Knowing God's WISDOM (Romans 16:27) lets me rejoice in His plan for my life.

Knowing God's GOODNESS (Ephesians 2:7) lets me get in on His mercy, love, kindness, and grace.

Knowing God's GLORY (Psalm 19) lets me appreciate all of His creation and how I personally fit into it all. It is that Glory of God, when worshiped, which becomes our glory. "Christ in you, the hope of glory." (Colossians 1:27).

If you want to know God, there is no other way but to worship Him. Two specific chapters in the Book of Revelation, 4 and 5, tell us how to worship the Lord. In verses 9 through 11 of chapter 4, we are given a threefold description of worshiping God.

1. There must be a FALLING DOWN (verse 10). Five times the Bible commands us to humble ourselves. Don't wait for God to do it. Do it yourself! It is in this act of humbling ourselves that God reveals Himself to us. It is perfectly said in the song: "When I survey the wondrous cross/On which the Prince of glory died,/My richest gain I count but loss,/And pour contempt on all my pride."

No worshiper of Jesus Christ can stand straight in His presence. We must become as little children, willing to see our prideful selves broken. We must no longer brag about our works for God, but rather consider His dealings with us.

2. There must be a CASTING OF CROWNS BEFORE THE THRONE (verse 10). A crown is an instrument that exalts the wearer. Steve Bartkowski has had several crowns.

God has given him many gifts. You, too, have many crowns in your life, specific things that bring compliments to you. There are God-given areas in each of our lives, but no true worshiper of Jesus Christ takes the glory for them. Apart from God you have nothing. Why should we take the credit for things that are not really ours?

God does not want us to deny having these talents, but wants us to be sure that they are put before the throne. This means they are recognized as being owned by God and not by us. It also means that God could touch them in an adverse way and we would not question Him in doing so. We must have an open hand in all of our dealings with God. If He has given you a gift, thank Him for it and acknowledge that it is His.

3. There must be the TELLING THE LORD HIS WORTH-SHIP (verse 11). Why tell Him if He already knows? Remember, that whatever we worship, we become like. God will reveal His character to those who acknowledge Him in all their ways. As we worship Him for who He is, we will find ourselves becoming like Him. This demands becoming quiet in His presence, where we can adore Him, being fascinated by Him, and admiring Him for who He is. Don't allow any portion of Scripture to escape your study. Read it all and read it often. God has revealed Himself to you in the pages of His Word.

It is this deep knowledge of God that Steve and Sandee are presently seeking. Their concern is that this book will be a means of getting you to know God in a greater way than ever before. It is also their purpose that for those who read these pages, this book may cause them to get their lives right with God.

Do you know God? Do you really KNOW Him?

CARL A. RUDISILL LIBRARY
LENOIR RHYNE COLLEGE

CAL LIBRARY
E COLLFY

10

Encouraging One Another

To the degree a man has laid down his right to himself, to that same degree he will be an encouragement to others. It is impossible to reach out to another when we are preoccupied with ourselves. The greater our preoccupation in knowing God, the greater will be our ability to meet the needs of the body of Christ. No one can encourage as God can! It is the very self-giving attitude which Jesus possessed that is the very essence of Christianity and of building up His children.

"Bear one another's burdens," says the Apostle Paul, "and thus fulfill the law of Christ" (Galatians 6:2). Paul is saying that the law of self-giving is the law by which Jesus lived. People today believe that spirituality comes in many different, calculated forms. It does not! No one is more spiritual than the one God has worked into a spirit of "denying self for the sake of another."

Paul found it a delight to give himself for the brethren. He said of Timothy, his student in the faith, "For I have no one else of kindred spirit who will genuinely be concerned for your welfare." It was Jesus who "emptied Himself" for us. It was Paul who "poured himself out for us." It was Epaphroditus who "risked his life for the brethren." The early church was built on this solid foundation: "Do nothing from selfishness or empty conceit, but with humility of mind let each of you regard one another as more important than himself."

Jesus taught us how to function as a body. He was a great burden bearer. He still is constantly putting Himself under our load. He takes on Himself the burden of our sins. He takes on

Himself the burden of our restlessness, saying, "Come unto me, all ye that labour and are heavy laden, and I will give you rest" (Matthew 11:28 KJV). From the manger to the cross, this offering up of Himself for us summarized His life.

The question that needs to be asked the recipient of God's offering for us is this: "Are we so much greater than our Lord that we are above taking on another's burdens?" If this was the main characteristic in Christ's attitude toward us, does it not follow that His life in us will manifest the same attitude toward others? Of course it does! There is no possible way for a man to say he is right with God and refuse to weep over, get interested in, and take on the burdens of others.

To have the mind of Christ means to minister to even the "least" of God's children. Matthew 25 tells us that in heaven we will be rewarded for doing various deeds in the name of God. We may not know it was to God, but God has said, "Whosoever has done it to the least of these my brethren, has done it unto me already!" (*see* verse 40). Have you ever "emptied" yourself on behalf of another?

Superspirituality is nothing but pious pride. It is encouraging men to look at us. It is even demanding that they do so or we will be upset! True humility does not care if we are noticed; we just find ourselves getting on with God's business for other people. How do we fulfill the law of Christ? The answer is not to gain super knowledge and live all our gifts to the fullest. The answer given already is to bear one another's burdens (Galatians 6:2). If He laid down His life for us, we ought also to lay our lives down for the sake of the brethren (*see* 1 John 3:16).

Too often, Christians put little protective coverings around themselves and try their best to look like first-class saints, as if they hadn't a single problem in the world. Their unwillingness to expose themselves for who they are and their refusal to share their failures produces a self-centered life-style. With their eyes on themselves, they begin to drift and after a matter of time, they drop out of the race. "It is too hard to keep living the life," they say. It is not too hard, it is just that no man was meant to do it alone!

Expression in the Christian life demands that we be set free. Christ came to do just that. If we understand our position in Christ as was mentioned, it will produce freedom. If we grow to really know God, it will increase freedom. If we continue in His Word, it also will produce freedom (John 8:32). True brokenness and humility means that we are "willing to be ruled." God delights in seeing this attitude because then, and only then, can we minister as God would have us. God has a lot to say through us to others. How many of us are ruled by God to the point that attitudes and conversations help to pull others out of bondage?

The rapid growth that Steve Bartkowski made in his early Christian life is due to the intense fellowship that he experienced. Fellow Christians on the team came to his rescue along with a few others outside the team. Steve's associations had to be carefully chosen at the beginning, because it was natural that people acted concerned for his Christian life, when what they really wanted was just to meet him. This problem was remedied when God brought some key people in his life who lived the attitude shared in this chapter. It was not the amount of people that created such a "growing" atmosphere for Steve, but it was the quality of their lives before Him. Some people can be with you for two hours and project more of God than others can for days.

Steve shared this with me recently. "There is no way a guy could grow in the Christian life as I have without the intense fellowship I have known." He went on to share with me what he meant. "I have met people who have been ten and twenty years old in the Lord who do not seem to have a grasp on the Christian life and its importance as I have. I attribute the reason for that to be mainly the quality of people God has brought into my life." We were chatting together and I asked Steve who the individuals were who were influential in helping him to grow so fast. Steve began to share with me, "Dan, you were the greatest stabilizing force in my life. It is because of your teaching and patience with me that I grew as I have." I was thrilled to hear the compliment, but I know it took many others besides myself to contribute to Steve's growth. My role just happened to be that of Bible teacher after he met the Lord Jesus Christ. Other people have still a greater private ministry with Steve; not the least to mention is, of course, his wife, Sandee.

June Jones's friendship with Steve has had the biggest impact of any one man on the team. Steve said to me, "June is the most real and honest person I have ever met. We happen to have the same likes and dislikes and on top of that, we are both quarterbacks." It is as though the Lord arranged June to be Steve's counter-quarterback, just to befriend Steve in areas that no one else could identify with. People would normally expect rivalry between two contending quarterbacks. It is to this normal expectation that the power of the Gospel has dealt a severe blow. God changed all that "expected" conflict and made them the best of friends with a genuine love for one another. "June's attitude is that if he doesn't make the Atlanta Falcons, then the Lord must have something better for him. Don't get me wrong, he puts forth the best effort. But his security is obviously not in football but in Christ."

I have been in prayer meetings with several of the team members. At one point during the preseason, the three quarterbacks were praying for one another. Scott Hunter, June Jones, and Steve Bartkowski began to pray. They knew that one of the quarterbacks would more than likely be cut from the team. Steve's position was secure, but the others could have been cut the next day. To listen to Steve and June pray for one another and thank God for their friendship through the past season was a thrill. I remember June and Scott praying, "Lord, thank You that if the only reason You sent me to Atlanta was to meet these brothers in Christ, it was worth it all. I am now ready to go if You say go." These kinds of prayers certainly would baffle the world's thinking. Most people cannot imagine being that selfless and free to share it openly in prayer like that.

Steve went on to say, "Of the other guys on the team, Greg Brezina and Ray Easterling have had the greatest impact on me." Even before Steve was a Christian he commented, "Their brotherly love for each other made me really see a difference in Christianity. I would see them truly care for one another and share with one another on a different level than I had ever seen. I wanted this same kind of relationship with someone."

Steve recalls how Greg was always the strong spiritual "daddy" to the team. Most of us know that it was Greg who hung in there when there were no Christians at all on the team. It was Greg who encouraged the new Christians on the team to build up one another. His burden is obvious to every one of the Christians on the team. Ray Easterling became next in line to lead the team in this close spiritual unity. "When you match Ray's discipline with his heart for God, you really have a combination," Steve said. Greg and Ray are the best of friends and it is amazing to know that their friendship with each other was used so mightily in showing Steve the way to be intercepted by Christ.

Two very special people in Steve's life are Tom and Frieda Courson. They are a couple in Atlanta who Steve says, "Pulled me through some of the toughest times of my life." Especially during the season, their home became a haven for Steve and Sandee. They would go and relax and watch a couple who know God and know how to glorify Him. Tom with his kindness and calmness and Frieda with her clear insights from the Lord, gave Steve and Sandee real direction for their lives. "When my attitude was bad, they would shake me out of it and point the way to where God wanted me in my witness for Him," Steve said.

Of the Christians on the team, there is a variety of spiritual growth. Never a dull moment for me! Some, like Greg and Ray, are able to teach me. Others, like Billy Ryckman and Wallace Francis, are beautifully teachable and quite young in the Lord. The amazing work of God is that one-third of the team at the time of writing this book professed to know the Lord personally. As far as we know, that is the largest group of Christians on any NFL team in the league.

Steve said, "We are a tight group of believers during the season. Whatever concerns another brother becomes the immediate concern of ours." It is true, they are like the ideal picture of what church fellowship should be during the preseason and the regular season. Last year, every night the guys would meet together in Steve and June's room to pray and share the Word of God. To see big men humbled before God was a testimony to God's power alone. To see them sensitive to one another's burdens was a testimony to God's character in them.

The world often blames the poor games on the fact that too many teammates were Christians. Some said, "If they were less interested in Christ and more in football, they would win." Well, the world has to have something to talk about and blame for team losses. A personal meeting with any of the Christian players will reveal that they are motivated men. They are the men who know the importance of playing football just like their passion after God. There is no dichotomy between Christ and football to them. They don't just pray that they will be men of God; they pray also that they will be the best football players in the world.

God only knows the impact that so many of the Christians on the team have had on Steve. We were tempted not to mention them, but the point must be made that it was the individuals with their own personalities yielded to Christ that made the impact they had: Greg Brezina with his father image that brought stability to the team; Ray Easterling with his discipline in football and Christianity; Brian Cabral with his sensitive kindness in word and deed; Bob Glazebrook with his calmness in going through difficulty; Lewis Gilbert with his encouragement of others when he himself was hurting. John James with his openness to the Lord and his constant interest in others' success; June Jones with his ability to let you be yourself, failures and all; Ron McCartney with his security in the Lord and not people; Tom Moriarty with his childlike faith and determination for the Lord; Billy Ryckman with his simplicity in the faith; Paul Ryczek with his kindness and consistently strong attitude for God; Dave Scott with his big body and equally large heart for the Lord; Wallace Francis, who has received many a pass from Steve, and is growing in the Lord like few men around; and Jay Shoop, who is an encouragement to all the team through being a trainer and brother in Christ.

These are some of the brothers who have to one degree or another shaped Steve into a man of God. Some have had greater impact than others, but God will reveal in the end the contribution they have made to him and to the Lord because of it. When we lost two "brothers" last year to other teams, Scott Hunter and Ralph Ortega, the team knew they had a double responsibility. They must now pray for God to use the two who left, and He is, and they must ask God to fill their vacancy with new Christians, and He did that, too!

There is a desire now, like never before, among the Christians to reach out and let their light shine for the sake of all the other players. They know it is not in their talk but in their walk that others will see Christ in them.

No one can understand the intense unity of the team until they see how cold professional football can be at times. Seeing that it is 100 percent individual performance over another guy, it is very difficult, apart from Christ's bond, to overcome selfish attitudes. The players battle with this every year and God bonds them together every year. I cannot imagine the free reign the devil himself would have in attitudes alone on the team if God had not gotten hold of some of the key players. Don't get me wrong—the Christians on the team still fail and sin and sometimes blow it badly. They are not supersaints! God has not grown them up overnight and some are still struggling. The thrilling part is that they know this and therefore, they have bigger hearts than they have heads.

Most of us know that fertilizer is good for plants, and yet too much will kill them. Too much can burn them out. The church today and Christians in general, have frequently been guilty of feeding the young Christians too much too fast. There is a need to bring a sense of pace into their lives. It is encouraging each other and bearing one another's burdens that does this. Just listening to sermons about God, without pouring our hearts for God, will work against us. The world many times has accused Christians of not being spiritual enough. God is in control of this and He grows people better than any of us can.

The guys prayed for another member of the team one time, "Lord, because we believe it is Your will, we would ask that You exalt our brother Tom. Give him a chance to give You glory through such a victory in his life." These guys pray like this because they truly love to see God exalt one another. I have seen Greg come into the Bible study in tears because of his burden for others. His openness began to encourage others to be open, also.

The art of encouraging one another can be just another spiritual commandment unless we grasp how to do it. The following are phrases that the Christian world ought to get familiar with and begin using around each other. Find me a place where they are used much, and I will show you fellowship and unity like nowhere else.

1) "Forgive me" or "I have sinned, will you forgive me?" 2) "I need your help." 3) "What can I do for you?" 4) "Thank you; I appreciate you very much." 5) "Your life is an encouragement to me." 6) "What can I pray for in your life?" 7) "Would you pray with me about something?" 8) "I want you to know that I really love you." 9) "Without you a large part of my life would be hurting." 10) "I believe you are the best friend a person could have."

All of these phrases are illustrations of expressing the heart. Many times we want to say something to a person who means much to us and we don't, because society has told us that it is not "cool." God loves His children to talk to one another with their hearts, truly expressing what they feel in a positive way. Encouragement demands that we change our vocabulary many times. The "What's happening?" kind of communication might have to change to "What can I pray for?" kind of communication. The key is that we truly do accept one another (Romans 15:7); that we be devoted to one another (Romans 12:10); that we honor one another (Romans 12:10); that we admonish one another (Romans 15:14); that we serve one another (Galatians 5:13); that we bear one another's burdens (Galatians 6:2); that we bear with one another (Ephesians 4:2); that we submit to one another (Ephesians 5:21); and that we encourage one another (1 Thessalonians 5:11).

Steve told me one time that he thought God would take them to the Super Bowl someday. I asked him why he felt that way. He said, "I just know that they will ask me on national television if this is the greatest moment in my life, and I will have the joy of telling them that it cannot hold a candle to the day I met Jesus Christ." It is this witness for the Lord that might be the glory God is looking for. Either way, God is going to get glory from Steve Bartkowski's life. It is a walking testimony of God's power, presence, and provision.

I must admit that even this adventure we have shared in writing this book has brought us closer than brothers. Steve keeps telling me the influence I have had on his life, but his kindness and patience with me has been a testimony to behold. He has said many times, "God's glory is what matters, Dan. Just enjoy writing the book and leave the results to God."

11

Be a Disciple, Not a Disposal

There is no question in the Word of God on the issue of discipleship. But there was a question in Steve's mind about it. He was hoping that God would just pour His knowledge into him simply by wishing it so. There were those who encouraged Steve to get into a discipleship program, but he had to see the need for himself.

It was a rainy morning that Steve and I had planned on meeting at a private airport in Atlanta. We were to fly to Rome, Georgia, to speak at a college there. Steve was going to give his testimony, and for a change I was not going to do much speaking. I was mainly going along for the ride and for the purpose of encouraging Steve.

Steve knew he was to share what God was doing in his life, but his quiet personality made it difficult for him. He would always say to me, "Dan, I'll just share for a few minutes and then you take over." I did not mind that, because he was the best listener to my messages of anybody in the world. He would just sit on the edge of his seat and open up to all that God would say. But this particular time he was all alone. He was to share not only a testimony, but an up-to-date account of what God was doing in him. I could tell he was unusually concerned.

As it happened, the rainy weather kept us from flying to Rome. We were stuck with driving there. We were disappointed because of the time it would take, but God soon showed us the reason. We were not on the road very long before Steve began to share his deep concern. His concern soon changed to conviction and then conviction changed to tears.

He said to me, "I know I am not growing as I should. There are areas in my life I know are not right and I am not allowing God to correct them. I even know what I must do, but have not been willing."

Inside of me, as Steve continued to talk, was a bursting heart of gratefulness. Steve cried and I rejoiced. He did not know I was rejoicing, of course. I just let him continue to talk about his frustration with the Christian life and his failure to appropriate what God was wanting of him. I was grateful to God for this frustration because I knew that only God could get Steve ready to be discipled. People had talked to him, his wife had encouraged him, I in the past had lectured him, but only God could work the desire deeply into him.

I was aware that Steve was having problems in the Christian life due to lack of discipline. He was hoping to cruise into the knowledge of God. His frustration became clear when he found himself more of a disposal than a disciple that day with me in the car. When I speak of a disposal, I mean a Christian who takes in information, but only grinds out the same lifestyle.

Steve went on to say, "I feel like my life is grinding up some spiritual truth, but I am not producing anything worthwhile. I don't want to find myself a year from now a fruitless, faithless Christian." He kept talking and I kept listening. I suggested nothing for the longest time. Then Steve finally caught on to my silence.

He said, "DeHaan, I know what you're thinking."

"Yes, you probably do," I said.

"You have known that I should be in a disciplined study of the Word and you've waited on me to see the light."

"That's a pretty good assessment of my thoughts," I replied.

The conversation continued and finally Steve said, "I am ready for anything you can offer. It does not matter what you come up with. I will do whatever you suggest to get me and keep me in shape spiritually. I have no desire to stand in front

of people and speak about things I am not even living myself."
He said, "What do you suggest, Dan?"

I cannot tell you the thrill I was experiencing. It is one thing
to disciple someone, but quite another for one of your best
friends to ask you to disciple them. I went on to tell Steve,
"Brother, you only have two choices. You are definitely saved,
so now you can be a disciple or a disposal. You can become
strong enough to lead others and feed others, or you can drink
in limited truth, grind it up, and put out limited action. You
can press on to maturity as Hebrews 5:14 and 6:1 speak of or
like Demas, you can love this present evil world and by taking
it in, become a disposal" (2 Timothy 4:10).

By the time we reached Rome, Georgia, to speak, Steve was
a new man. He had given in to what God had been working on
for a long time. The timing was perfect. Now I knew that he
really wanted the cream and not just the milk. I knew now that
whatever I felt was of God for him, he would back me up. The
next step was up to me!

On the way home from the meeting, Steve told me that he
would definitely pray about going through a discipleship study
with me and would let me know in the next two days. From
our conversation together, I knew what his answer would be,
but to seal it in prayer now was good. Two days later Steve told
me, "I'm ready for the challenge." He said, "I know you are
busy, Dan, and cannot give me the time it would take, so we
will have to tailor-make this study for your sake."

"I have a lot going," I said, "but I will cancel those things if
you are serious about this."

I knew the ball was now in my court. I had to rearrange my
schedule and get off for a day of prayer to seek God's face on
what God wanted Steve to know and do at this point in his life.
Some people would say, "Did you have to go on a day of
prayer to find this out? There are books galore on discipleship
that would be good for Steve." This would normally be true, I
suppose, but I am a firm believer that we cannot disciple indi-

viduals with any mechanical program. People are different and those we get close to in a one-to-one relationship should be given the consideration of our adapting truth to their needs. Also, I am a firm believer that we are giving the average person we disciple too much information. We are overequipping them! They become highly qualified to be utterly useless! They learn things they are incapable of even doing something about. We then educate them into ignorance and sometimes even into arrogance.

The art of discipleship is the art of raising proper questions and then dealing with them. This was Jesus' method. He did not just give out information. He raised serious questions through giving "reality" exams; exams that were needful for where they were in their spiritual lives. As we expose people to reality and raise questions, then and only then do answers fit and become valuable. A disciple is not one who knows facts that can be passed on to others. He is one who identifies himself with God's interests in himself and other people. A disposal can grind up information and pass it on. Usually the information is dead, decayed, and dry; but it is still passed on. A disciple is one who follows so closely to the Lord that His passion as well as performance comes through.

It is so easy for any of us "teachers" to get into the habit of thinking that because we are teaching the masses, we are doing God's will. We begin to professionalize our performance and lose the passion of it all. It was to Spurgeon, who at the age of nineteen filled the church with five thousand people twice on Sunday, that a man made a critical comment. He said, "I am a pastor and I don't have a big church like you do. You have the power to do so much more because of the size of your church." Spurgeon, with all of his insight, said, "Sir, you are not responsible for how many, but for what kind!" The truth of this statement is profound, to say the least. The Bible makes it clear that all spiritual leaders, even evangelists, are responsible for what kind, not how many (Ephesians 4). Most people today believe that leadership is for the evangelical extrovert. In discipleship we are to identify, not just grind out information or put on a performance.

Spiritually, as adults we are not just to feed babies, but produce adults for the purpose of having babies. It is one thing to stand up and feed others, and quite another to reproduce life through your own identification with another person. This is the goal of discipleship. Everything else is a giving out of words that basically cost us little in doing so.

I went off for my day of prayer and on that day out in the woods, the Lord made it clear to me what I was to do with Steve. The day I went away was characterized by on-and-off rain. The sun would shine and then rain would fall, back and forth. It was through understanding the pattern of the weather that God confirmed an idea to me. The personal goal with Steve was to make him consistent and persistent when things are going well and when things are going badly. What Steve needed was to understand how to endure for the Lord. God showed me the purpose and the goal in discipling Steve when I turned to Philippians 1:27–30. Later, Steve agreed that this was his desire and determination.

That day of prayer was a momentous occasion. I asked God to give me a clear plan of action so I could disciple a person and not tell him too much . . . rather, not overequip him. I was aware that I had to keep the plan down to limited meetings because the Falcons' football schedule was about to begin. Minicamp was about to take place and time was at a premium. I only had a couple of months now to see Steve respond to this. What I did not realize was that two other key players were going to ask me to disciple them, and they did not even know I was doing this with Steve. Both Wallace Francis, 1979's most valuable player for the Falcons, and Billy Ryckman, the little yet tough wide receiver, asked me on two separate occasions only days after the day of prayer to teach them the basics in the Christian life. I had to adapt what I was doing with Steve for them, but the plan God gave on that day was the need for them, also.

Finally, Steve and I sat down to go over what I had planned. He was as excited about this as anything I had ever seen. In fact, Steve is so even tempered that I thought he just did not get overly excited about anything. I was wrong, because as I unfolded this plan of discipleship to him, he just affirmed to me over and over that this was exactly what he needed. So we began!

In this first session, after we had had a season of prayer, I shared with him the schedule and the commitment this would take for both of us. I warned him that the devil would see to it that our times together would be difficult to keep. How true this would become! I then gave him what I felt was the outline of needs in his life before he would become a spiritual leader of men.

Our conversation went something like this: "Steve, I have broken up this plan of discipling you into ten sessions. We will cover one truth each session that will last about an hour and a half, and then you will have about five hours of homework to do in between sessions. It will require a lot of reading and searching the Scriptures to find the answers. It will cost you about two hundred dollars for books before I am through, and we will need to meet at least once a week."

My next statement was, "Are you ready for this?" He replied, "More than for anything I've ever done." Again it was confirmed to me that God had prepared Steve for becoming a strong disciple and discipler of men. His interests began to change. I found him telling me things that required much discernment. Many times I was taken aback by the intensity of his statements. It showed me that he was personalizing the truth and that the truth was moving him to action. His messages began to have greater authority. This was the thrill of it all to me. You could tell he was not saying just words now, but expressing a life-style. The authority of a man who knows and is knowing God came through. He was growing! I was thrilled!

The plan I came up with for Steve is listed here. I list it because this plan might be one that many of you could use or adapt for yourself. I would suggest that if there is a doubt as to whether you are growing spiritually or if there is a lack of authority in your life, that you carefully check yourself against these principles.

The ten sessions are listed below along with their subtopics. The applications to them and the Scriptures to support them are found in the following chapter.

1. **Conversion:** This involves having a clear understanding of repentance, faith, and assurance.

2. **Christian Life Overview:** This involves having a clear understanding of how God's plan of redemption affects us personally.

3. **Discipleship:** At this point we go into the meaning of commitment under the Lordship of Christ.

4. **The Word of God:** There must be an understanding of the authority and trustworthiness of Scripture, how to study the Word, and how to meditate upon it.

5. **Obedience and Warfare:** This session demands a clear explanation of the life of faith. The attacks of the wicked one are explored with a specific look into the warfare of the mind.

6. **Prayer:** Effective praying is studied, along with determining God's will in life through prayer.

7. **Fellowship:** This demands a clear understanding of what real fellowship is. The importance of "share groups" and "accountability groups" are emphasized. Weekly group Bible study and understanding the purpose of the church is also to be the life-style of one who understands the need for fellowship.

8. **Worship:** This missing ingredient of the Christian life is to be given handles for a sturdy grasp. Worship is studied with the view in mind of making a man "endure as seeing Him" (*see* Hebrews 11:27).

9. **Attitude Transformation:** The Be-attitudes are studied and their applications given to daily living. Understanding life

under the sovereign control of God and how praise fits into the Christian's life is carefully discussed.

10. **Personal Evangelism:** The simple sharing of one's faith is discussed. The purpose of this study is to make a person creative and sensitive to the needs of others around him.

These are the ten categories of study that Steve and I went through. My idea with each of these topics was to make them clear enough to Steve so that he could teach them to others on the team or within the church. If these ten topics are gone into with much study and prayer, they will produce a stretching of faith. They will "disturb" a man into action. Comfort breeds carelessness! A true disciple of our Lord Jesus Christ might face real difficulties, but the sin of apathy will be cured forever. The end result of any discipling is to ignite the soul of a man.

The Lord Jesus lived in a spiritual state of tension. Even in His last moments before the Crucifixion, He passioned His way in prayer while His followers slept. The church today seems to be a sleeping church. Our goal in discipleship is not to add to that number but to raise up men and women who through their life and lips will shake the church so that the church can shake the world.

One of the books that I gave Steve while discipling him was the book called *Spiritual Leadership* by Oswald Sanders. In that book, Sanders quotes Samuel Logan Brengle, whom I have enjoyed reading. He was a great leader of the Salvation Army and a great motivator of men. He spoke these challenging words to Steve and to all of us who have "ears to hear."

Leadership is not won by promotion, but by many prayers and tears. It is attained by confessions of sin, and much heartsearching and humbling before God; by self-surrender, a courageous sacrifice of every idol, a bold, deathless, uncompromising and uncomplaining embrace of the cross, and by an eternal, unfaltering, looking unto Jesus crucified. It is not gained by seeking great things for ourselves, but rather, like Paul, by counting those things that are gain to us as loss for Christ. That is a great price, but it must be unflinchingly paid by him who would be not merely a nominal but a real spiritual leader of men, a leader whose power is recognized and felt in heaven, on earth and in hell.

I remember when Steve read those words and the other statements in the book on leadership qualities. He called me on the telephone just to tell me that he was disturbed over the demands of being a spiritual leader. He said, "I never knew that spiritual leadership was so different from natural leadership." I knew the Holy Spirit was getting through in making Steve a leader among men when he said this. Natural leadership causes one to lord it over another, while spiritual leadership causes one to cry out, "Lord, help me!"

The leadership Steve was beginning to discover was the same that David Brainerd discovered when he wrote in his diary:

> Farewell vain world, my soul bids you adieu;
> My Saviour taught me to abandone you;
> Thy charms may gratify the sensual mind;
> But they cannot please a man for God designed.

Steve's present walk with God is confirming the fact that God is making him a mighty leader for His own glory!

12

A Strategy for Living a Committed Christian Life

The Christian life is a marathon run. It is not a one-hundred-yard dash, nor is it a football game where you can soon stop or huddle up for a new start. The Bible speaks much about endurance as the difference between a leader and a follower. To endure demands that we be in shape, and to get in shape demands that we exercise. To exercise we must have a plan and our plan must be put into a scheduled program. According to Hebrews 5:14 this is the way to run the Christian life.

I personally have thought that the old story of "The Hare and the Tortoise," or a similar story, should have been in the Bible. I know of nothing that gets the message of Christianity across more clearly. You remember the story, don't you? The hare and the tortoise begin a race together. The hare immediately jumps ahead and runs for all it is worth. Finally the hare realizes it has such a lead that it stops to rest. While the hare is in its sleepy condition, the steady and consistent tortoise passes it. In the end, the slow but sure plodding of the tortoise wins the race. This is like the Christian life!

Steve Bartkowski had to experience this. Endurance is the key to being a spiritual leader. In order to endure we must be in shape, and it takes an entirely different kind of conditioning to run long distances than to run the length of the football field. Along with his football career, Steve now had to learn to run marathons for the Lord.

Leadership is made up of men who know the road, who can

keep ahead, and who can pull others after them. The late President Truman's definition of leadership was: "A leader is a person who has the ability to get others to do what they don't want to do, and like it."

An old Chinese leader was asked about leadership. He responded, "There are only three kinds of people in this world—those who are movable, those who are immovable, and those who move them." A spiritual leader is a mover of men through the power of the Holy Spirit. He does this leading by example and not by political power play. He is never a dictator, but a director. He is not a soloist for the Lord, but a co-laborer who leads and needs others.

It is probably safe to say that a spiritual leader is one who has no desire to lead, but is forced into it by the pressure of the Holy Spirit because of the need of the hour. A man is not a leader by virtue of his position, but by his performance. A man can have a title on his life, but just as anyone can put a label on an empty bottle, a title may be given to an empty life.

One of my favorite Scripture verses that describes the Christian life as being a marathon race is found in Hebrews 12:1–3. " . . . let us also lay aside every encumbrance, and the sin which so easily entangles us, and let us *run with endurance the race* that is set before us. . . . For consider Him who has endured such hostility by sinners against Himself, so that *you may not grow weary and lose heart"* (my italics). There seems to be an increasing number of anemic Christians of late. Harris polls tell us that 50 million people in America alone claim to be Christians. For this nation to be in the shape it is in tells us this statement is either not true or else the majority is being led by the minority. Those who know better have no power to lead those who don't know better. The blind are leading those with clear eyesight, because those with sight are too out-of-shape to keep setting the pace.

How we lead others and thereby run this marathon race of endurance is determined by our goals. The goals we choose are determined by our priorities. Whether or not we reach our goals is determined by our planning. Our plans must then have a strategy that causes us to live life to the fullest and lead others in doing the same.

The ten-session plan I took Steve through was a plan of leadership. He knew my goal for him was to reproduce life in someone else. If I could teach him how to run the endurance race, then he was to do the same. Information alone will not do it. It will take the pain and the time of seeing the spiritual truths come alive, not just on paper, but in a living human being.

The following strategy was developed for Steve Bartkowski. I would encourage you to take the pain of developing your own spiritual muscles through exercising yourself with these principles. I must warn you to take your time. These ten sessions were done over a long period of time, and they should be with you. You cannot glean the most from these ten sessions if you are in a hurry. Always remember, a man who waits on God loses no time.

In the following discipleship plan you will notice each session has a *goal* and a *plan of action*. Within the plan of action there are several varied requirements. These requirements are important to reach the goal, but they *must* be personalized. Your plan may vary from this, but be sure it accomplishes the goal listed.

Session 1—CONVERSION

The Goal: That one would be able to express to another person his own assurance of salvation based on personal faith in Christ and promises from the Word of God.

The Plan: (1) Explain the following words, *and* list *two* Scripture verses in explaining each one (Repentance, Faith, and Assurance). I had Steve do this alone and then we would share the answers together. He had two pages of information on these three key words in the Bible. He also wrote down about five verses on each. Steve said, "This is a great thrill—to find out the Bible speaks so directly to so many issues." (2) Read

the page entitled Study Sheet #1 at the back of this book. (3)
Be prepared to tell me how you know you are a Christian. (4)
If you only had five minutes to give a testimony, what would
you say? On this fourth requirement I wanted Steve to be able
to take one minute on his past, two minutes on his conversion
experience, and two minutes on what God has done since then.
I told Steve, "So many people share twice as much about their
preconversion days than what God has done since. The end
result is that the devil gets more glory than God." (5) Be prepared to tell me where restitution fits into the Christian life.
This is for the purpose of knowing how to handle past failures.
(6) Read chapter 6 of *The Lost Art of Disciple Making*, by
Leroy Eims. (7) Read chapters 10 and 11 in the book *Basic
Christianity*, by John R. W. Stott. (8) Read the book *How
Come It's Taking Me So Long to Get Better?* by Lane Adams.

I knew after this first homework assignment that God had
begun to make Steve a leader. His hunger grew and his knowledge of God grew equally. We were ready now for the second
session.

Session 2—CHRISTIAN LIFE OVERVIEW

The Goal: That we would be able to understand the great doctrine of salvation and how it affects us personally.

The Plan: (1) Be sure to understand the following words well.
(Justification, Redemption, Forgiveness, Reconciliation, and
Sonship). These are the key words that God uses to describe
our spiritual relationship with Himself. We had nothing to do
with receiving the gift of these five words and the full intent of
their meaning. I can remember so well the moments Steve and
I shared together on this session. He had again done more than
I asked for his homework. He said to me with great confidence,
"JUSTIFICATION means just-as-if-I'd never sinned." He
then gave Deuteronomy 25:1 and Romans 8:33 to support it.
"REDEMPTION," he said, "means freedom secured through
payment of a price." He used four verses to prove this:

1 Corinthians 6:20; Ephesians 1:7; Revelation 5:9; and Mark 10:45. "FORGIVENESS means God cleared the debt I owed because I repented." Psalms 103:12; Colossians 3:13; Matthew 26:28; and Colossians 2:13 were given to support this. "RECONCILIATION means I was an enemy and was brought near like a friend." Romans 5:10,11; 2 Corinthians 5:18; and Colossians 1:21,22 were the verses used. Last, Steve said, "SONSHIP means to own all that God owns." He had Romans 8:14,16 and Ephesians 1:5 to explain it.

I share all this with you at this point to let you know that Steve was doing his homework with great enthusiasm. The hunger was remaining. This is the thing to look for as we lead others!

(2) Read the outline on Study Sheet #2. (3) Be able to explain the above five words. Those five key words are words used often by Paul in his writings. Romans 6 gives the truth of our salvation in many unique ways. (4) Memorize 1 Corinthians 10:13 and Galatians 2:20. (5) Read chapter 5 of *Keys to Spiritual Growth,* by John MacArthur, Jr. (6) Read *Principles of Spiritual Growth,* by Miles Stanford. This is an excellent book, right to the point for this session. (7) read *Birthright!* by David Needham.

Session 3—DISCIPLESHIP

The Goal: To evidence the Lordship of Christ by understanding commitment to Christ, and by committing at least one previously uncommitted area to Christ.

The Plan: (1) According to Luke 9:57–61, list what commitment is NOT. (2) According to Matthew 10:37–39, list what commitment IS. (3) Be sure to study and understand the truth of Philippians 1:27–30 and 2 Corinthians 2:14–16. (4) Read *Spiritual Leadership,* by Oswald Sanders, especially chapters 10 and 11. (5) Read through 2 Timothy and look for the marks of a committed man. (6) Read *Knowing God's Will and Doing It,* by Grant Howard.

Session 4—THE WORD OF GOD

The Goal: To know the authority of the Word along with proof of its trustworthiness. To know how to study the Bible, how to meditate upon it, how to memorize it and thereby glean the most from it.

The Plan: (1) List two or more verses in the Bible that prove the Word of God is inspired and inerrant. (2) Read chapters 2, 7, 10, and 11 of *A General Introduction to the Bible,* by Geisler and Nix. (3) Be able to tell why just the 66 books of the Bible are inspired. (4) Be able to define inspiration clearly. (5) Read chapter 2 of *The Battle for the Bible,* by Harold Lindsell. (6) Read chapters 7 and 8 of *The Joy of Discovery,* by Oletta Wald. (7) Be able to tell me how to study a book in the Bible. (8) Read *How to Study Your Bible,* pages 17–19, by Kay Arthur.

It was in this session that I taught Steve what tools to use in getting the most out of studying the Word of God. The key ingredients are a good concordance, a good Bible dictionary, a good word-study book, one good commentary on the whole Bible, and a Greek lexicon.

Session 5—OBEDIENCE AND SPIRITUAL WARFARE

The Goal: To cause the person we disciple to understand how to walk by faith and how to take up his cross daily and follow the Lord. This should be evidenced by carrying out specific applications in the Word of God and by trusting God through a difficulty in his or her life.

The Plan: (1) Define the words *obey* and *spiritual warfare.* (2) Study Genesis 3:1–5 along with Ephesians 6:10–20 for insight into the ways of the devil. (3) List the methods of the devil and then list the spiritual weapons and what they mean. (See Study Sheet #3 at this point.) (4) Be prepared to discuss personal "rights" in relation to obedience. (5) Read Study Sheet #4. (6) Read Romans 14, 15 and 1 Corinthians 12–14. (7) Read C. T. Studd's Biography, written by Norman Grubb. (8) Read *True Discipleship,* by William MacDonald. (9) Read *The Christian Soldier,* by Martin Lloyd-Jones. (10) Read *Why Revival Tar-*

ries, by Leonard Ravenhill. This book is a must! Optional book: *The Power of the Spirit,* by William Law.

Session 6—PRAYER AND DEVOTION

The Goal: That one would demonstrate consistency in his prayer life and give evidence that he *prays* prayers and doesn't just *say* prayers. There should be active participation in prayer groups and a knowledge of what it means to pray with passion. There should be a consistency in his or her quiet times with the Lord.

The Plan: (1) See Study Sheet #5 at this point. (2) Study the prayers of the Apostle Paul in the New Testament. (Colossians 1:9–12; Ephesians 1:16–19; Ephesians 3:14–19; and Philippians 1:9–11.) (3) List the direction, by way of priorities, that Paul's prayers take as an example to follow. (4) Study what the Bible says will happen to a person who fails to pray (Study Sheet #6). (5) Study these five passages in order to find the five great "negatives" to prayer. In other words, what will happen if you fail to pray? (Luke 18:1; Luke 22:40,46; James 4:1–3; 2 Timothy 1:3; and Acts 4:31.) (6) Trust the Lord to answer one specific prayer and share the answer with someone. (7) Read the book *Prayer,* by O. Hallesby. (8) Read *Revival Praying,* by Leonard Ravenhill. (9) Begin to use the "2959 Plan" notebook. It is a daily prayer guide that, in my mind, is the most effective prayer tool today. It can be obtained through Agape Ministries, P.O. Box 6006, Titusville, Fla. 32780. (10) Read *The Kneeling Christian,* by an unknown author, published by Zondervan Publications. (11) Read *A Treasury of Prayer,* by Leonard Ravenhill. Optional reading: *Morning and Evening,* by C. H. Spurgeon and *My Utmost for His Highest,* by Oswald Chambers. These are both devotional books to be used in a daily reading method.

Session 7—FELLOWSHIP

The Goal: To experience true unity and expression in the body of Christ. There should be active participation in "accountability groups" or "share groups" along with expression within the body of a local church.

The Plan: (1) Seek an active open relationship with another Christian of the same sex. Ask him or her to join you in a ministry of encouraging one another. (2) Read *Building Up One Another*, by Gene Getz. (3) Begin to seek others to join you in an "accountability group," a group of Christians dedicated to building up one another on a weekly basis. (4) Read *Let God Love You*, by Lloyd John Ogilvie. Make applications to yourself and share them with those in your "accountability group." (5) Do a study on the word *fellowship* from the Epistle of 1 John. Make a note of its meaning along with the fourth and fifth chapters of Ephesians. (6) Read *The Church—The Body of Christ*, by John MacArthur, Jr. (7) VERY IMPORTANT: If you are not in a church where they are feeding you and you are not able to use your gifts, then seek out a local fellowship where you can.

Session 8—WORSHIP

The Goal: To know what it means to be fascinated with the Person of God and to adore Him above any earthly comfort or comrade. To actively seek time to get alone with God for the purpose of telling Him His worth.

The Plan: (1) Study the importance of worship through the following passages: Jeremiah 9:24; Hosea 6:6; Exodus 33; Hebrews 11:24–27; Luke 10:39–42; Revelation 4 and 5. (2) Read *The Pursuit of God*, by A. W. Tozer. Read this book carefully! (3) Begin to discipline yourself to come into God's presence and wait on Him without listing prayer requests. (4) Read *The Knowledge of the Holy*, by A. W. Tozer. (5) Read *Knowing God*, by James I. Packer. (6) Begin to use the book called *The Christian Book of Mystical Verse*, compiled by A. W. Tozer. This book is a great aid in worship. It lists a number of old poems and hymns without the music. Many hymnbooks can have a similar effect on the worshiper. (7) All of Oswald

Chambers' books, of which there are more than thirty, are extremely good for those who desire to know how to worship the Lord. His emphasis and explanation of being in love with Jesus Christ is very timely. My favorite of his is *Conformed to His Image.* Optional reading: *God, I Want to Know You,* by Dan DeHaan.

Session 9—ATTITUDE TRANSFORMATION

The Goal: To be able to see a change in our attitudes toward those around us. To watch God root out selfishness and pride from our hearts. To make the Be-attitudes a way of life in every area of participation.

The Plan: (1) Begin memorizing the Be-attitudes in Matthew 5:3–12. (2) Study Ephesians 4:1–3; Philippians 2:3–11; and Romans chapter 12. In studying these passages, make notes on attitudes that need changing within your life right now. (3) Read *The Sermon on the Mount,* by Oswald Chambers. (4) Read *Studies in the Sermon on the Mount,* by Martin Lloyd-Jones, especially pages 42–148. (5) Read *The Autobiography of God,* by Lloyd John Ogilvie. (6) Begin to concentrate on what it means to live under the sovereignty of God. Apply God's sovereignty to all areas of your life and make note of at least one area where the knowledge of God's sovereignty causes you to think differently about that area. (7) Read *Spiritual Problems,* by Oswald Sanders. (8) Study Romans 8:28; Psalms 37:4; 2 Chronicles 20:15. (9) Begin to exercise *praise and thanksgiving* in everything and note the difference it makes. (10) To understand the meaning of *praise and thanksgiving,* study 2 Chronicles 20:21,22; Isaiah 61:1–3; Romans 5:2; 1 Peter 1:6,7; James 1:2–4; Jeremiah 29:11; and Psalms 50:13–17; 22,23. (11) Read Study Sheet #7.

Session 10—PERSONAL EVANGELISM

The Goal: To take the initiative in sharing the Gospel clearly, using the Word of God. To be free from self to the degree that

God's interest in other people becomes your interest. To be bold in knowing whereof you speak concerning the plan of salvation.

The Plan: (1) Be creative to begin with and develop your own style for the plan of salvation. Write down what must be told a person for salvation to take place, and then put it in your own words for someone on the "street" level. (2) Begin to make a list of non-Christian friends with whom you would like to share the Lord. (3) Read *Born to Reproduce,* by Dawson Trotman. (4) Read *How to Give Away Your Faith,* by Paul Little. (5) Read *The Church at the End of the Twentieth Century,* by Francis Schaeffer. (6) Read *The Master Plan of Evangelism,* by Robert E. Coleman. (7) Begin the habit of having on your person at all times some kind of literature that could be left with someone or that would help you lead someone to Christ. This little failure is often the cause of many missed opportunities for the Lord. (8) Go witnessing on the streets with someone in your "accountability group" or with a friend. (9) Begin to make sharing the Lord a way of life. Think of your life as a builder of other lives. Whether Christians or non-Christians, you should have a freshness from your walk with Jesus Christ. If you are around a person for several minutes or hours, you should be able to turn that conversation around to the things of God. MAKE THIS YOUR CONSTANT GOAL! Don't allow your life to remain in the "holy huddle" with exclusively Christian fellowship. Be sure you are touching the needs of lost men.

Study Sheets

Repentance

Webster's definition: To feel sorry.

The word in the verb form is found in Luke nine times—in Acts five times—in Revelation twelve times—in 2 Corinthians 12:21.

Metanoeo = *Meta/Noeo*—To perceive after.

To change one's mind or purpose—always used in the New Testament for good. Used 108 times in the Bible in one form or another.

Theologically, the word means "That change wrought in the conscious life of the sinner, by which he turns away from sin."

It has three elements:

1. Intellectual—A recognition of sin involving personal guilt (knowledge of sin).
2. Emotional—Change of feeling, godly sorrow, not just remorse and despair. Psalms 51:2, 10,14; 2 Corinthians 7:9,10; Matthew 27:3; Luke 18:23.
3. Volitional—A change of purpose—a seeking of pardon and cleansing. Jeremiah 25:5; Psalm 51; Romans 2:4,5.

According to Scripture, repentance is wholly an inward act. Confession of sin and reparation of wrongs are fruits of repentance.

True repentance never exists unless it is in conjunction with faith. Luke 13:1–5; 15:7.

The greatest story of repentance is in Luke 15:17–32.

Repentance is to be done in three areas:

1. Repentance toward God. Repent of running our own lives and going our own ways, independent of God and thinking it right to do so. Acts 20:21 and Acts 8:22.

 2. Repentance of individual sins and attitudes. Five of
    seven churches in the Book of Revelation were told to
    repent.
 3. "Repent from dead works" (*see* Hebrews 6:1).

Psalm 51 shows us that true confession involves a right view of
sin, a right view of God, and a right view of self.

 1. Right view of sin: A recognition that sin deserves judg-
    ment.
     a. Psalms 51:1, "Have mercy upon me" (KJV).
        Justice: Getting what I deserve.
        Mercy: Getting less than I deserve.
        Grace: Getting none of what I deserve.
     b. A recognition that sin demands cleansing. Psalms
        51:2.
     c. Accepting full responsibility for it. Psalms 51:3–5;
        58:3.
 2. Right view of God: David in Psalm 51 cites several at-
    tributes and characteristics of God and draws practical
    applications from them. God's holiness, for example,
    requires "truth in the inward parts" (Psalms 51:6 KJV).
     a. Confidence in God's power to take care of sin.
        Psalms 51:7.
     b. God's chastisement. Psalms 51:8.
     c. His forgiveness. Micah 7:18.
 3. Right view of self. David recognized he must live a
    holy and godly life.
     a. For the sake of the sinner. Psalms 51:13.
     b. For the sake of God. Psalms 51:17.
     c. For the sake of the saints. Psalms 51:18; 66:18.
                   Woe is me
                   Lo, I am cleansed
                   Go tell the world

                                       See Isaiah 6

STUDY SHEET #2
The Message of Faith

Introduction: What was it that made Paul so stable?
1. He was absolutely sure he was in Christ.
2. He was absolutely sure what he had in Christ.
3. "In Christ" used 130 times in his letters.

I. Passages dealing with our position in Christ.
   A. Ephesians 1:3-14 (praise for spiritual possessions).
      1. We have purpose, verse 4 "chose."
         a. Aortist tense, "Once for all."
         b. (ek) preposition, "Out of."
         c. Middle voice, "For one's own self."
         d. Chosen out of the world, once for all, to be God's own treasure.
      2. We have a prospect (foretaste, anticipation, outlook). Verses 5, 6.
      3. We have pardon (redemption). Verses 7, 8.
      4. We have power (revealed in Word). Verses 9, 10.
      5. We have plenty (full supply or abundance). Verse 11.
      6. We have peace (sealed with the Spirit). Verses 13, 14.
         a. We are His—ownership.
         b. We are safe—security.
      7. We are prayed for. Verses 15-23.
   B. Colossians 2:9-15.
      1. In Christ is "perfect" fullness.
      2. In Christ is "permanent" fullness.
      3. In Christ is "practical" fullness.
         a. We are complete in Him. Verse 10.
         b. We are circumcised in Him. Verse 11.
         c. We are created anew. Verses 12, 13.
         d. We are cleansed in Him. Verses 13, 14.

II. Purpose of our position in Christ.
    A. Confidence. Philippians 1, Acts.
    B. Character. Colossians 3:5–17.
    C. Capacity for service and intake.

III. Power of our position.
    A. The exercise of our position. Philippians 4—power of choice.
    B. Exhortation of our position.
        1. Errors in misunderstanding it. Colossians 2:16–23.
        2. The "I am, I do" principle. John 15.

STUDY SHEET #3
Spiritual Warfare

(Ephesians 6:10–21)

The methods Satan uses: 1) He lies. 2) He is an accuser. 3) He is a disturber. 4) He is an aggressor, that is, he moves fast. As we will see from this study, those who are right with God, he hits the hardest. 5) He is a deceiver. 6) He is a disputer. He will dispute the Word of God and minimize it, saying, "That doesn't really apply to you." He will say, "Don't be concerned with that truth in the Word of God. You haven't grown that far yet. It is not expected of you to live it yet."

1. How do we defeat the devil when he comes to us as a *liar?* *See* verses 13 and 14: "Wherefore take unto you the whole armor of God, that ye may be able to withstand in the evil day. . . ." The "evil day" refers to periods of months and even years when the devil attacks us, oppresses us, hits us from all angles, when devotions are not interesting, when we can't seem to break through to God. WE COMBAT HIM AS A LIAR TO US. "Stand therefore, having your loins girt about with truth . . ." (KJV). The only way we combat this attack is by putting on the BELT OF TRUTH. This belt is the Person of Jesus Christ. Jesus Christ made the statement in John 14:6, "I am the way, and the truth. . . ." Our whole method of defeating the evil one is based on Jesus Christ holding all our armor together. He has already defeated the devil. God wants perfect, spontaneous, on-the-spot obedience to be your first reaction. This is basic! When the Person of truth, Jesus Christ, tells you to do something, whether it is in His Word or clearly given through other means, DO IT! If you don't, you are open to the wiles of the devil, for you have dropped your sword because the belt of truth was off.

2. When the devil comes to us as an *accuser,* how do we defeat him? Verse 14: ". . . and having put on the breastplate of righteousness." The devil is a tremendous accuser. THE DEVIL WILL DEFEAT OUR EMOTIONS BY ACCUSING US. He comes and says things like this: "Listen, compared to these other people, you're not much spiritually. You might as well give up; you're not growing in the Lord very fast. Look at this or that person. You don't match up to his spirituality." Our emotions will sink to the bottom when the devil accuses us. We cannot stay on top and defeat the wicked one, if he is accusing us, without the BREASTPLATE OF RIGHTEOUSNESS. The breastplate is this: I don't measure up, but Jesus Christ does. There is nothing that the devil can accuse Jesus Christ of, and if I am perfectly related to Him, he can't accuse me.

3. How do we defeat the devil when he comes to us as a *disturber?* Ephesians 6:15: "And your feed shod with the preparation of the gospel of peace" (KJV). Having feet shod with peace is living an adequate life all the time, having all that I need. I'm sure you have heard the illustration of the man who was going to cross over a frozen part of the Mississippi River. He began to walk over it slowly, when he heard a crack. Immediately, he got down on his hands and knees. Then all of a sudden he heard this very loud noise and he looked behind him—a huge truck was crossing the ice. The man picked himself up, looked straight ahead, and skipped across the ice. This is peace— knowing that Jesus Christ has the ice so thick that when the devil comes to put a crack in it, it can't hurt it in the least. The devil would love it if he could get me to crawl around as though the ice is weak or cracked. He would love to back me up into a corner and have me to be afraid of him. Peace is having the assurance of God to such a degree that nothing can scare you or hinder you from that effective moving on in the Lord. Don't let the devil back you up into a corner. Let him try what he wants to but keep that peace constant.

4. When he comes to us as an *aggressor,* how do we defeat him? Ephesians 6:16: "Above all, taking the shield of faith . . ." (KJV). What is the shield of faith? When the wicked one comes to us as an aggressor, just in simple faith lift your life to Jesus Christ. Every time I take the fiery temptations of the devil to Jesus in simple faith, He puts them out. Faith is powerful; don't ever minimize it. Faith is not jumping to conclusions. Faith is coming to the conclusion that you are going to jump. The shield of faith can be used as an armament of aggressiveness. Christians are sitting around today scared stiff of the devil's attack. The early church had an aggressiveness. They weren't shouting, "Look what the world has come to." They were shouting, "Look who's come to the world." Jesus Christ is your righteousness, and He never retreats from the devil. He has got him beat in every way. In simple faith, claim His righteousness and you will defeat him.

5. How do we defeat him when he comes to us as a *deceiver?* Ephesians 6:17: "And take the helmet of salvation. . . ." The helmet of salvation cannot be broken. The Christian is the only one who can be attacked on all sides and still have an upward look. Nobody can stop that upward look to Jesus Christ. "Look up for your redemption draweth nigh" (*see* Luke 21:28). If the devil can get you to look at results, or look at all things he is doing, or look at problems, he will love it. I can't have my eyes on the Lord and on other things, too. Even if the devil can keep you looking at him, he knows that is better than looking up to the Lord.

6. How do we defeat him, when he comes to us as the *disputer of the Word of God?* Ephesians 6:17: ". . . and the sword of Spirit, which is the word of God." The Word of God has the same effect on the devil as the Roman sword had on a man. Every time we win a victory by using the Word of God, we have a major part in destroying him. This is why we should be

memorizing the Scripture as much as possible, so we can have this aggressive weapon always ready to defeat the wicked one in our lives. With the shield of faith and the sword of the Spirit, we aggressively attack the devil instead of having him attack us.

The Question of Personal Rights

Romans 14–15; 1 Corinthians 8–10; 6:12,19,20. The above passages clearly set forth the Christian's position in regard to "questionable practices."

The principles obtained from these passages are as follows:

1. SELF-DENIAL FOR THE SAKE OF OTHERS. This attitude must be in the life of a committed Christian. We are not here to receive, but to serve.

2. CAN YOU DO IT FOR THE GLORY OF GOD? 1 Corinthians 10:31. God is to receive glory through our actions.

3. DOES IT HURT YOUR CONSCIENCE? Romans 14:22, 23 speaks of a God-given conscience to the Christian. It acts as a monitor for what is right and wrong.

4. DOES IT HURT YOUR BODY? 1 Corinthians 6:19,20 tells us that our body is the "house" of the Holy Spirit. This does not mean that the body is to be kept from difficulties or hard work. We can get in shape to the point where those difficulties are taken well. It does mean that what is harmful, especially to the "inner man," should be avoided.

5. IS IT EXPEDIENT? 1 Corinthians 6:12 speaks of what is "profitable" as being what we should be doing. Some things are good but they may not be the best. We should try to be at the place in the Christian life where we exercise what is best and not settle for only the good.

6. WILL IT CAUSE ENSLAVEMENT? 1 Corinthians 6:12 also speaks of Paul's determination to not be mastered by anything except the will of God. If what I am doing is causing enslavement to it, then it is wrong.

7. WILL IT EDIFY? 1 Corinthians 10:23 speaks of the fact that the Christian should build up others around him. If

what we do does not help but rather hinders another Christian, it is wrong.

8. ARE YOU AN EXAMPLE TO FOLLOW? Paul said, "The things ... seen in me, practice these things. ..." We are to set the pace for others, not follow behind.

9. DOES IT EXERCISE YOURSELF TO BE THE MAXIMUM FOR GOD? Hebrews 5:13,14 speaks of a self-imposed training program to train our senses to discern good and evil.

STUDY SHEET #5
Persistence in Prayer
(Colossians 4:2–6)

1. THE SPEECH OF PRAYER: Prayer is the most important speech your mouth will ever utter. "Prayer is the nearest approach to God and the highest enjoyment of Him that we are capable of in this life."

Colossians 4:2: "Stay at it." Ephesians 6:18; 1 Thessalonians 5:17; Luke 21:36; Acts 6; Romans 12:12.

HAVE A GOD-CONSCIOUSNESS: Bringing everything that happens into view of God.

Greek for "devote" is *proskartareo:* It means "super strong and super steadfast."

Luke 18: Persistence in prayer illustrated.

Luke 11:5–13: PERSISTENCE IN PRAYER ILLUSTRATED.

Prayer is dangerous: We must submit to the consequences of its answer.

DON'T EVER PRAY A PRAYER THAT YOU ARE NOT PREPARED TO BE THE ANSWER TO.

PRAYER IS REBELLION AGAINST THE STATUS QUO—4:2: "To accept life as it is is to surrender the Christian view of God" (David Wells).

Rebellion in prayer resists any authority in control but God's.

Powerful prayer only flourishes where there is a twofold belief: 1) that God's name is hallowed too irregularly; and 2) that God Himself can change this situation.

To pray with devotion means you enter into the fact that God and this world are at cross-purposes. To "sleep" or to "faint" is to act as if they are not.

"Remaining alert" comes from the *gregoreo,* meaning to be vigilant: Don't go to sleep during prayer and pray according to priorities.

Thanksgiving: This is the fifth time it is mentioned.

2. THE SPEECH OF PROCLAMATION: Verses 3,4; Ephesians 6:18–20. "A door of utterance": Paul had no negative
   circumstances, only unique opportunities. The first prayer
   in the early church was for boldness. Acts 4:29; Revelation
   3:7,8.

Prayer

God always answers prayer in one of four ways:

1. **YES:** Often God will give us what we request immediately. We should rejoice when this happens.

2. **NO:** In 2 Corinthians 12, God gave Paul a "no" answer to prayer. The test in our lives is whether we can rejoice over God's "no" as much as over God's "yes." Remember, God gave both of them. If it is from His hand, it has to be right. James 1:17.

3. **WAIT:** John 11 records the story of Lazarus' resurrection. God made them wait on this miracle for the benefit of many.

4. **SOME OTHER WAY:** God will often answer a prayer that you pray, but He will do it another way than you thought. This way, only He gets glory and it tests your motive in prayer. If you wanted it just your way, then you will become proud when the answer comes or defeated when it does not. King David is an illustration of this. He wanted to build a temple. God did not let him, but he built the best temple in the world through the writing of the Book of Psalms.

THE FIVE NEGATIVES TO PRAYER:

1. PRAY OR YOU WILL FAINT: Luke 18:1
2. PRAY OR YOU WILL FALL: Luke 22:40,46
3. PRAY OR YOU WILL FIGHT: James 4:1–3
4. PRAY OR YOU WILL FORGET: 2 Timothy 1:3; 1 Thessalonians 1:2
5. PRAY OR YOU WILL FEAR: Acts 1–6; 4:13,31

The Be-Attitudes

Introduction:

All the commands in the Sermon on the Mount mean absolutely nothing without the Be-attitudes in the first 12 verses. (Read KJV.) Unless you "be" something, you can't "do" anything.

If the Be-attitudes are not our *character*, then the rest of the Sermon on the Mount will not be our *conduct*.

Every one of the Be-attitudes talks about the *condition of happiness created by the character of the Be-attitudes.* (Remember: God does not create happiness by new surroundings, He creates new surroundings by happiness.) The only way God has planned for us to be happy, no matter what circumstances we have, is to be living the Be-attitudes daily.

THE BE-ATTITUDES
(Keep in mind their order)

"Blessed are the poor in Spirit" HUMILITY Proverbs 8:13; 16:5; 18; 26:12 29:23; Psalms 101:5

This is the first character God builds into the life of a disciple. It means YOUR LIFE IS AN OPEN BOOK. YOU ARE WILLING TO BE RULED. God builds it into you by a *crisis, valley,* and by *exposing your faults.*

The OPPOSITE of humility is PRIDE

"Blessed are they that mourn" MOURNFUL	This means to have God's view on self, sin, and service. It will result in a BROKEN HEART in your service and attitude.	The OPPOSITE of mourning is lack of purpose, lack of seriousness, lack of prayer, BOREDOM.
"Blessed are the meek" MEEKNESS	This means not impressive, not sensitive; you can take criticism.	The OPPOSITE is self-pity and anger or greed.
"Blessed are they which do hunger and thirst" HUNGER FOR HOLINESS	This means you long to be positively holy; hungry to know God's Word.	The OPPOSITE is lack of spiritual desire, apathy, irregular devotions.
"Blessed are the merciful" MERCIFUL	Those who fully forgive all who offend them and *return* love and understanding.	The OPPOSITE is bitterness and resentment.
"Blessed are the pure in heart" PURE IN HEART	Those whose motives and desires are under the control of Christ.	The OPPOSITE is impurity. Impurity is a character more than a conduct.
"Blessed are the peacemakers" PEACEMAKERS	Those who make things right with everyone they have wronged.	The OPPOSITE is a condemning attitude or a guilty conscience or both.
"Blessed are they which are persecuted" PERSECUTION	Those who identify with Christ so closely that those who reject His principles will reject them.	The OPPOSITE is compromise of standards and fear of witnessing.

Books to Read
For Study Sheets

(*See* Chapter 12)

The Lost Art of Disciple Making, Eims, Zondervan/NavPress, paper, $3.95.

Basic Christianity, Stott, Eerdmans, paper, $1.95.

How Come It's Taking Me So Long to Get Better?, Adams, Tyndale, paper, $3.95.

Keys to Spiritual Growth, MacArthur, Revell, Cloth, $4.95.

Principles of Spiritual Growth, Stanford, Back to the Bible, paper, $1.25.

Spiritual Leadership, Sanders, Moody, paper $2.95.

Knowing God's Will and Doing It, Howard, Zondervan, paper, $4.95.

A General Introduction to the Bible, Geisler and Nix, Moody, cloth, $11.95.

The Battle for the Bible, Lindsell, Zondervan, paper, $4.95.

The Joy of Discovery in Bible Study, Wald, Augsburg, paper, $2.95.

How to Study Your Bible, Arthur, Reach Out, $2.00.

C. T. Studd, Grubb, Christian Literature Crusade, paper, $2.50.

True Discipleship, MacDonald, Walterick, paper, $1.25.

The Christian Soldier, Lloyd-Jones, Baker, Cloth, $8.95.

Why Revival Tarries, Ravenhill, Bethany Fellowship, paper, $2.95.

The Power of the Spirit, Law, Christian Literature Crusade, paper, $2.00.

Prayer, Hallesby, Augsburg, paper, $1.50.

Revival Praying, Ravenhill, Bethany Fellowship, paper, $2.95.

2959 Plan, Agape Ministries, looseleaf notebook, $4.75.

The Kneeling Christian, Author Unknown, Zondervan, paper, $1.95.

Treasury of Prayer, Ravenhill, Bethany Fellowship, $2.95.

Morning and Evening, Spurgeon, MacDonald, $10.95.

My Utmost for His Highest, Chambers, Dodd, Mead, & Co., Inc., Cloth, $5.95.

Building Up One Another, Getz, Scripture Press, paper, $2.75.

Let God Love You, Ogilvie, Word, paper, $3.95.

The Church—The Body of Christ, MacArthur, Zondervan, paper, $2.50.

The Pursuit of God, Tozer, Christian Publications, paper, $1.95.

The Knowledge of the Holy, Tozer, Harper & Row, paper, $3.95.

Knowing God, Packer, InterVarsity Press, paper, $3.95.

The Christian Book of Mystical Verse, Tozer, Christian Publications, paper, $3.50.

Conformed to His Image, Chambers, Christian Literature Crusade, paper, $1.75.

God: I Want to Know You, DeHaan (available January 1982), Moody Press.

Studies in the Sermon on the Mount, Chambers, Christian Literature Crusade, paper, $1.50.

Studies in the Sermon on the Mount, Lloyd-Jones, Eerdmans, Cloth, $11.95.

The Autobiography of God, Ogilvie, Gospel Light, Cloth, $9.95.

Spiritual Maturity, Sanders, Moody, paper, $1.50.

Born to Reproduce, Trotman, Back to the Bible, paper, $.75.

How to Give Away Your Faith, Little, InterVarsity Press, paper, $3.00.

The Church at the End of the Twentieth Century, Schaeffer, InterVarsity, paper, $2.50.

The Master Plan of Evangelism, Coleman, Revell, paper, $1.95.

Birthright!, Needham, Multnomah Press, cloth, $8.95.